STAND OUT

By
Jade Hicks

Copyright © 2018 Jade Hicks

All rights reserved.

ISBN: 172045468x

ISBN-13: 9781720454687

Table of Contents

INTRODUCTION 1

PART 1: AN INTRODUCTION TO BRAND BUILDING 3
   ARE YOU LEAVING MONEY ON THE TABLE? 5
   CREATING A STAND OUT BRAND:
   HOW WILL IT GET ME NOTICED? 13
   HOW YOUR CLIENTS BUY 19

PART 2: YOUR BRAND FOUNDATION 25
   WHAT IS A BRAND? 27
   POSITIONING 33
   BRAND CELEBRITY 39
   JADE'S STAGES OF BRAND CELEBRITY 45

PART 3: WHAT IS THE PURPOSE OF YOUR SHOOT? .. 51
   WHAT ARE YOU SELLING? 53
   WHO IS YOUR CLIENT? 57
   HOW DOES IT LOOK RIGHT NOW? 63
   STEP OUT OF YOUR BOX 65

PART 4: INTRODUCTION TO PHOTOGRAPHY 69
   THINKING ABOUT PHOTOGRAPHY 71
   CONNECTION 79
   PHOTOGRAPHY AND STORYTELLING 85
   WHAT IF YOU DIDN'T USE IMAGES? 91
   WHAT YOU NEED VISUAL IMAGERY FOR! 95

PART 5: HOW TO USE YOUR IMAGES 101
   HOW TO USE IMAGES ON YOUR WEBSITE 103
   HOW TO USE IMAGES ON YOUR SOCIAL MEDIA 107
   HOW TO USE IMAGES ON PRINTED MATERIALS 117

PART 6: PLANNING YOUR PERSONAL BRANDING PHOTOSHOOT **125**

    PREPARING FOR A BRAND SHOOT 127

    HOW TO COMMUNICATE WITH YOUR CREATIVES ... 141

PART 7: MEET THE WOMEN WHO MADE SIX FIGURES FROM THEIR SHOOTS **151**

    Linda 153

    Bunmi 157

    Vanessa 161

STAND OUT BRANDS - OVER TO YOU!! **165**

INTRODUCTION

Hello Fabulous!!

Although it may seem like a minefield to get noticed in an industry of thousands, it is actually not that difficult to create a brand that STANDS OUT and connects directly to your dream clients. Even though there is a wealth of advice, tips, strategies and systems to get your business visible, I am lovingly providing you with my personal tried and tested approach that works with you and your biz from the ground up - growing and evolving your brand, as you and your business move onwards and upwards.

In creating this book, I have drawn on my vast experience and knowledge of building a brand that STANDS OUT and helps cement your legacy in a way that feels authentic, easy and most importantly, true to you and your story.

This book, or visual branding 'bible' as I like to call it, is separated into actionable sections all supported visually as well as with written steps, so you can really understand the IMPACT your brand visuals, photography and graphics, can have on your dream clients.

I want this branding bible to help you long after you have created and designed your brand. I have meaningfully created it so you can put to use the techniques and processes whenever your brand needs anything from a small tweak to growth in a completely new direction.

Being a creative, visual impact seeking person, I love working on hands-on projects. I hope you feel like I am right there with you, helping you with all your soul searching, deep digging, brand creating and communicating right from the start.

Whether you are:

- Rebranding and looking to reinvent yourself, reflecting the transformation and business growth you have been through, or...
- Ready to launch and needing help expressing your individuality, making a strong brand statement and creating a STAND OUT online presence, or...
- Renewing your confidence in yourself and your business by experiencing a transformation to feel unstoppable...

...You **need** more than a here today gone tomorrow Brand Identity. You need a full Brand Makeover!

So, Legacy builder, lady boss extraordinaire, what are you waiting for?

Let's get this branding party started!

PART 1

AN INTRODUCTION TO BRAND BUILDING

CHAPTER 1

ARE YOU LEAVING MONEY ON THE TABLE?

So, before we enter into the first section of this book I need to address some of the common denominators I come across when working with Fabulous Lady bosses on their brands. I have created a quick reference list for you to use as a starting point, to help identify where you brand is struggling, and what action needs to be taken to move you from Drab to Fab and get you on the right track right now.

The first question is...

1. Is your brand losing you money?

We probably all recognise this scene... we are happily scrolling through a social platform and we can all relate to when that moment hits. You know the moment:

That split-second decision you make to STOP mid scroll.

A post *stops you in-your-scroll*. It instantly grabs your attention and makes you *physically* break your habit. It changes your behaviour from queen of scrolling, to stopping and taking notice of what you have just seen.

Now the fact that you have scrolled past at least ten other posts very similar in content and message to this one which has **stopped** your scroll-a-thon doesn't for one millisecond resonate with you as a consumer. You have no idea that you have missed 10 other opportunities to connect with people or businesses with a similar love, passion, desire or message, all you know is: This post!

This post that made you stop, look up and take note.

So, what was it that did this? What made this magical act happen? And how many times do you think your ideal client, your perfect partner, your dreamiest fantasy customer has scrolled past you without even noticing you exist?

Take a moment to think now, how many potential sales have completely been lost due to you not being impactful enough to stop the scroll?

So, is your brand losing YOU money? Let's move on to question #2

2. Is your brand telling your story?

Do you feel like the identity you have created for your business is telling a story you don't relate to? Maybe you feel like when you see your posts, or even your products and packaging that it doesn't really connect with you and your big vision? Maybe you know that you have created a persona that isn't authentic and more importantly doesn't connect with your audience?

Let's think of a little analogy here. Imagine you are looking for a new car, and you head off to the garage. Perhaps you visit a couple of different brands to compare the ranges. Let's suppose you are completely new to buying a car - maybe you've only ever had a car bought by your parents, or have shared a car with your other half. Maybe you've had a company car for years and never before had the chance to go and choose what to buy.

So, where do you go to buy this car?

Now, unless you are in the very small minority of people who literally want to go to *every* garage to compare the deal they are going to get, you are probably going to be drawn immediately to a certain brand.

Think - Why?

What is it about that brand that immediately commands your attention? What story are they telling that is drawing you in, even if you haven't ever had one of their cars before? During this comparison period, have you ever taken notice of WHAT exactly it is that makes you visit those specific brands? And perhaps more importantly, have you ever considered what it is that makes you NOT visit other brands?

Because a car is car. They have four wheels and they get you from A to B. We all know they have a range of different features - smart gadgets, slightly different aesthetic appearance, particular functions - the list is endless! But have you ever considered WHAT makes you turn your head enough to consider one car manufacturer over another? And even deeper than this have you ever considered what makes you return to a manufacturer you have previously bought from instead of another that may be more competitive on price and features?

Now let's put this into the context of you and your business.

Do you know what story you are telling to make sure your clients aren't even considering looking at another in your industry?

And more importantly do you know what story TO TELL to make sure your clients are ONLY looking at you?

Is your brand TRULY telling the RIGHT story? Let's get on to question #3

3. Can you see and feel a particular vision for your brand, but no matter how hard you work, what you put out there just doesn't resonate?

Have you ever looked at Pinterest, Instagram and other visually strong platforms, seen gorgeous brand boards, mood boards and graphics floating about and instantly thought "WOW, I love that colour scheme!" Or maybe you're often flicking through home decor books and paint charts, and just fall in love with one theme after another?

When I started out my business journey, I had this vision for my brand being a specific logo and colour theme. I was so rigid on it, I felt like I knew *exactly* what it needed to be and how I wanted it to look. I had found this gorgeous colour scheme online, and I just knew that was what I was going to use. When I launched it, I got so many compliments on how pretty it was and how lovely it looked. It was great.

Then, about six months into my first business after I had spent a huge number of hours on designing all my marketing - my graphics, having my logo made , finessing my brand - and invested a lot of money on it, I'm going to be brutally honest...

I wasn't getting the clients.

I was not getting the enquiries or the engagement I needed to sustain the investments I had made and meet the running costs of my business each month. I needed to do something to get the money flowing into my biz so what did I choose to do? Well, I chose to take it all out on me! I thought it was all my fault.... maybe because I had used the wrong colours. I had used the wrong logo. Obviously, my ideal clients didn't like the colours I had chosen from Pinterest. Or so I thought.

So, I then embarked on another mission of "rebranding". I got busy, not with clients (i.e. paying customers!) but with redesigning my colours; heading back to Pinterest and finding another quick fix colour scheme that was "working" for someone else, and, well yeah - put all the time and effort into this.

What do you think the outcome of that was?

YEP - Nada! I found myself in exactly the same situation I had been in the first time round, only now I was 12 months down the line from launch and still hadn't got the clients, but had twice as much money invested in the business, and twice as many knocks to my confidence.

I had not only lost a ton of money, but more importantly and crucially I had lost something never to be regained: TIME!

Can you see and feel a certain vision for your brand but no matter how hard you work, what you put out just doesn't resonate? Here we move on to question #4...

4. Does business feel hard and inauthentic?

Ask yourself, are you feeling like every day you are dragging yourself into the office or struggling to get into working on your biz? Is it becoming a chore to find the "right" words to say, the "right" posts to put out on social media, the "right" business events to attend? You originally thought being the boss would mean 'super flexibility meets amazing work life balance' but that just isn't the reality right now?

Does any of this sound familiar: Jumping on for livestream videos or interacting in social groups feels like trudging through mud. You would rather hide behind your sofa than do one more livestream video - you just can't get it together.

Maybe you have had a brand identity created and it just feels forced and unrelatable - you struggle to represent, and feel disconnected when you see it.

What is out of balance? Where is it going wrong that it is feeling forced and hard? Where are you hiding behind a mask or creating a front to your business that is not sustainable because it isn't real?

Does your business FEEL hard and inauthentic?

Here is a quick summary

....

Is your brand losing YOU money?

Is your brand telling YOUR story?

Can you see and feel a vision for your brand to be a certain way and no matter how hard you work what you put out just DOESN'T RESONATE?

Does business feel HARD and inauthentic?

....

If you can answer YES to any or even ALL of these questions, then you are DEFINITELY in the right place!

Whether you are:

- Just starting out - and you *know* the important of a great and authentic brand. You're focussed on getting it done right from the start, but just don't know where to turn to make your vision a reality.
- Rebranding - for growth or refreshing your brand to a more soul-reflecting and customer resonating experience. It's a minefield with so many choices to make and conflicting advice, you just don't know where to start.

- Renewing your confidence - in yourself and your business, by experiencing a transformation to help you feel unstoppable!

Now is the time for you to express your individuality, make a strong brand statement and create a STAND OUT online presence with killer visuals, photos and graphics.

CHAPTER 2

CREATING A STAND OUT BRAND: HOW WILL IT GET ME NOTICED?

If you're at the beginning of your branding journey, you might be a little unsure as to what branding is all about. Don't worry! You are in exactly the right place. In this next section, we're going to take a look at what creating a STAND OUT brand is going to do for your business. We're going to see just HOW branding can elevate you to the next level, and understand a bit more about the power of strong branding.

1. Branding = Ramped Up Recognition

Create a brand that is simple, yet powerful enough to impact the desired impression on the memory of your dreamy client, and you will be propelled to celebrity status. *BEING MEMORABLE **IS** WORTH MORE THAN GOLD!*

MINDSHIFT - BE REMEMBERED FOR JUST BEING THERE

Deciding to dedicate your business behaviour to the priorities and lives of your dreamy clients rather than your own ideals will secure you referrability and loyalty.

Ask yourself the following questions:

- Do you know the moments in your customer's life when they need you most?
- Do you dedicate any part of your experience to those moments?
- Will you be there?
- Have you really looked at the lives of your target market and understood where you are needed?

Think about your favourite premium chocolate. Consider a brand like Ferrero Rocher.

Now, you know that when you have a birthday or a celebration to buy a gift for, you are always able to rely on that chocolate to look the same way, taste the same way and evoke the same reaction from the receiver. You know that without a doubt, that chocolate is going to be well received by the intended because it is a reliable and recognisable brand. They have already achieved 'Ramped Up Recognition'!

The Bottom Line to Achieving Ramped Up Recognition:

Having a brand that customers / clients and consumers can recall as the go-to expert when needed means you have reached top of mind recognition level. This increases your return, loyal clients AND referral customers!

2. Branding = Triggers Trust

Crafting an expert presence creates brand reliability, validity and trust. Your dream customer is more likely to buy from you and your business when you appear professional, polished and true. We, as human beings, are hardwired to connect emotionally and those programmed reactions have a huge influence on our decision making.

> **MINDSHIFT - WITHOUT TRUST, THERE CAN BE NO SUSTAINABLE BUSINESS**
>
> Trust is the foundation of any strong,
> lasting and prosperous relationship.

Now, let's try something. Consider what made you choose your hairdresser.

- Why do you return for your next hair appointment to the same hairdresser?
- If at the first appointment the hairdresser had carried out a fabulous service and then the second appointment the hairdresser had cut off a lot more hair than you asked and TRUSTED them to cut off, how would this affect your relationship?
- Would you return to the hairdresser for a 3rd appointment?

Again, think about that favourite chocolate brand. If you unwrapped a chocolate to find they had completely changed the appearance and taste, or were using a different type of chocolate to what you had expected, how would this affect the longevity of your relationship with this brand? Would you return to buy another box after the disappointment of unexpected and substandard changes made to the product? Or would you seek out a new brand to fall in love with and promote to being your go-to chocolate brand?

The bottom Line to Triggering Trust is:

Create a brand that is reliable and dependable. A brand that looks professional and polished CONSISTENTLY, and which delivers the same feelings and experience Every. Single. Time. You need to enable your greatest fans to be able to have constant faith that you can ALWAYS deliver what they want to expect and receive from you.

3. Branding = Talks to Your Customer Directly (supports advertising)

Your branding works as an advertisement for your business. You build on this by choosing your dreamiest clients and then targeting them directly, speaking to them through your brand. Focus on the narrowing down your targeting range, so that you are able to create a clearly defined picture in the mind not only of your business, but also in the mind of your target consumers as to WHO you are able to serve.

> **MINDSHIFT - SHOW UP FOR YOUR TRIBE & THEY WILL SHOW UP FOR YOU**
>
> Speaking directly to the ONE person
> you are providing your service or product to
> will help ATTRACT more of that kind of person.

Speaking directly to your ideal client acts as a filtration device to the wrong types of customer, and saves you valuable time which otherwise might be wasted presenting your offering to people who do not have a need for it.

Let's consider the brand Harley Davidson.

Now, if you watch a Harley Davidson advert, it is very clearly talking to a certain type of person. It will resonate to a person who is seeking freedom and thrills; who wants rugged and rustic pleasure, passion, individualism and mysterious power. It uses the **emotions** connected to **experiencing** a bike to connect with this person. It builds trust with this person, by cementing the knowledge that by buying a Harley Davidson, you are joining a passionate family full of individuals just like you.

The brand promise is that you WILL experience the thrills and pleasure and freedom that comes from owning a Harley, and it will make you powerful. Price doesn't even factor into the decision-making process for the Harley Davidson target client - they feel LUCKY and privileged to have been able to buy the product. Harley Davidson make sure this is the case by restricting the number of bikes they produce.

The Bottom Line to Triggering Trust is:

Create a product / service that your ONE DREAM CLIENT *wants* to experience. A product that they have a need to be able to come back to time and time again, and make sure you 'show up' every single time. Know what they want from the experience and ALWAYS consistently deliver.

4. Branding = Inspires Culture

Many employees and even consumers, need MORE! They need a cause to get behind, a mission and a reason to get involved. They want to know what goals you want to achieve so that they can get on board, and feel the pride and work ethic you have created.

> **MINDSHIFT - Your brand should act as a shining beacon.**
>
> Your brand will call to your followers and raving fans, and act as an emblem to bring them together.

Let's chat about Twitter.

Twitter has become renowned for having a strong culture and following amongst not only its 330 million active daily users, but also within the employees of Twitter. Offering a team-oriented environment, supported by quirky rooftop meetings, friendly team members, free company meals, yoga classes and unlimited holidays, Twitter has inspired their workers to be motivated, and work towards company goals. Twitter employees genuinely WANT to be part of a company they believe is making a difference to the world.

The Bottom Line to creating a Culture that Inspires is:

Creating a happy, friendly and inviting feeling of community that your tribe WANT to be part of is prime - be they target customers, or employees and working partners! When people feel like they belong, and they are working towards and buying into a cause that fires them up, they feel fulfilled and purposeful in a natural and organic way.

5. Branding Generates Customers & Makes Money for your Business

By delivering on the promise of your unique experience, you are enabling your biz to capitalise on referrals from your customers. You are monetising the most profitable source of FREE advertising.

A strong brand is going to generate, and usually guarantee, future custom. The more time, energy and investment you make in developing and building your brand values, the better the financial return.

MINDSHIFT - INVESTING & DEVOTING TIME, ENERGY AND RESOURCES TO CRAFTING YOUR BRAND WILL REAP YOU THE BENEFITS FOR THE LIFETIME OF YOUR BIZ

**YES!!! I want to create a Brand that Stands Out
and get me and my biz noticed!**

CHAPTER 3

HOW YOUR CLIENTS BUY

Understanding HOW your clients buy is the key to great marketing. Getting this right can make marketing effortless and easy for you, and enticing and engaging for your audience.

> **MINDSHIFT - YOUR CUSTOMERS DON'T BUY YOU. THEY BUY THEIR HIGHEST VALUE**

The expression 'people buy people' is ringing through my mind as I write this section.

People DO buy people - they crave authentic and real connection to be able to make decisions. These decisions are made based upon the order of their values. So, how can you realise what the highest value of your dreamiest client is?

Fact: Our minds decide what to buy.

All of our human behaviour is driven by a need to avoid pain - to preserve our body and mind - and a desire to gain pleasure.

For example, I recently started to run again. I used to run before I had my daughter, and I loved the freedom and the sense of accomplishment (plus how much my butt stopped jiggling more and more after every run!). I recently picked up my running shoes again and, after not running for 4 years I really felt every...

single... stride!! But I did it. I persevered and went out time and time again until it became easier and I could run further.

Every time I went out it was an effort, mentally and physically. My shoes didn't fit as well as they used to and they hurt my feet the first few weeks, but I kept going because I wanted the rush of adrenaline that kicks in when you finish a circuit. I wanted that high that comes from knowing you have just pushed yourself and achieved something that took you by surprise. Yes, I endured pain - running in the rain, and shoes that rubbed my feet, but I knew that the pleasure which comes from completing the run and the sense of accomplishment and self-satisfaction was going to outweigh any suffering or pain.

This basic concept is the main motivator for every decision we make. To be able to use this information to help you with selling to your target market, you first need to identify exactly who you want to sell to!

I identify the pleasure that comes from the accomplishment of running, however not everyone will associate pleasure from running. For some people the pain of the running will far outweigh any ideals of pleasure. So knowing who you are talking to and what they associate with pleasure is the key.

In the next section I am going to show you what you need to ask in order to figure out exactly who your dreamiest client is, but first we need to consider a few other motivators for how your dreamy client is buying.

MINDSHIFT: YOUR TRIBE WANTS TO FEEL YOUR STORY

Our lives and cultures are composed of many overlapping stories. Your tribe are looking to invest emotionally and have their emotional triggers activated. Telling stories engages the sight, sound, taste and movement areas of the brain. They help us feel an experience without actually really feeling it.

Now, when I say 'telling a story' I'm not talking about writing the most romantic 300 page novel. It is about showing your authenticity, interacting with your audience and in turn creating a magnetic connection.

Every story needs to have an emotional centre, how you FEEL about the events you're describing. What motivated you, what caused you trouble or conflict? How did you feel about what was going on around you and how do you feel about it now? It is from creating this emotional connectivity that you will build trust and loyalty amongst your audience.

I love the saying "You have to be **interested** to be interesting." The bottom line is, if you don't put care, thought and love into your story, then why would anyone else?

> **Everyone has a storyteller inside them,
> and everyone has a story to tell.**

MINDSHIFT: YOU DO NOT NEED BELLS AND WHISTLES TO SELL YOUR OFFERING!

Your tribe are looking for simplicity. They want the answer and they want to know the easiest way to get it. The more you jazz up your offering with complicated jargon and decorative doilies the more you turn your ideal match off!

Give people the simplest solution. Create an easy to follow framework. Make it simple for people to connect emotionally to you, and then make it simple for them to BUY FROM YOU. Literally, you need to show them how you and your product can make it FOOL PROOF to help them with their problem in the quickest time possible.

So, I want you to think about your website for a moment. Do you have a clear and concise reason for people to be on your website?

Newsflash! Your website is NOT ABOUT YOU! No one goes there to learn you have three dogs and live in the country - your website is a TOOL FOR YOUR BUSINESS. Make it easy for people to emotionally connect with you, by using amazing images and photography on the pages they land on, and give them a simple and easy to follow call to action. Make it easy! Make it simple! Keep it streamlined.

Simplicity is the key!

MINDSHIFT: MAKE THE PROBLEM THE ENEMY, AND TEAM UP WITH YOUR DREAMY CLIENT!

I love this concept. The reason your business exists is to help to solve a specific problem.

So it's a no-brainer to show your allegiance with your audience AGAINST the problem.

So, your dreamy client will have a problem that they believe is the reason for all their woes. It is the reason their business is not growing, not moving forward, not doing what they want it to do. It is the reason the results are not as they want them. By aligning yourself with your audience AGAINST this enemy of a problem, you create a group of people who believe in the same thing. You can build a story, an explanation, which can unite a whole group of people. It creates a CULTURE behind your products and services and gets your audience excited to invest in them.

For example, I have worked with a lot of hair and makeup artists. Some who work in the commercial world doing catwalks, trade shows and displays etc. and some who work more domestically with weddings and makeover work. One of the fabulous makeup artists I worked with had a great concept that I thought was really clever around her marketing.

Now, it wasn't purposely done, she hadn't realised what a clever marketing technique she had created, it came completely from a place of authenticity.

She had a very strong belief and ideal over how makeup should be promoted and used, and also how it should *not* be. Her belief was around the trend of contouring. She had obviously worked in the industry a really long time, and she had carried out contouring and understood it, but she had a strong gut feeling that she just didn't *like it*. She believed it was creating a different face for her clients. Working in the wedding industry, although she wanted to make them the best they could be, she didn't want them to feel they HAD to be someone else. They had to have cheekbones and jawlines that looked a certain way, but her motto was all about ENHANCING and not covering or reconstructing.

So, by being strong in this belief she turned away a lot of work from ladies who wanted to have contouring, because she genuinely believes it to be the enemy. She felt contouring was making women even LESS confident with their makeup bags, and with their own faces, creating yet another media misrepresentation of the definition of "perfect", and how women 'should' look. She genuinely was completely against it, believing that even very young girls were learning it to be the norm, to be how they "should" look.

What her very strong views on the subject have actually done is attract a whole tribe of women who are anti-contouring. Women who believe you can use makeup to look the best version of YOU, to enhance your unique features rather than construct non-existent ones. It has created her a culture around herself, her business and her beliefs as a makeup artist and has meant she has a very STRONG tribe around her who believe the same thing. She united with them as one over this view on contouring.

Now obviously this concept has to be taken delicately. It is about small problems that people are experiencing, not politics, race or religion.

By utilising strong imagery, photography and visual graphics throughout your brand, and doing so CONSISTENTLY, you can tell the story, create the excitement and interest, connect to values and form an alliance with your dream client in the simplest and easiest way! By showing them who you are, what your brand is all about and how you serve them, you can solve their problem and fulfil their highest values.

All of which is achieved through GREAT photography and visual representation.

PART 2

YOUR BRAND FOUNDATION

CHAPTER 4

WHAT IS A BRAND?

According to popular definitions, a brand is:

"A type of product manufactured by a particular company under a particular name."

"An identifying mark burned on livestock or (especially in former times) criminals or slaves with a branding iron."

So, let's get REALLY clear on what a brand is not...

MINDSHIFT - A brand isn't one thing.

It's not a logo - This is a visual representation of the picture you want to create in the mind of your customers whenever they hear your name. It creates a consistent tie from your chosen colours to your full brand identity.

It's not a name - Although you want to be securely embedded in the mind of your target market, your name is just an identifying factor that brings your brand together.

It's not a business card - This is a supporting factor of your overall brand identity.

It's not a website - Your website works as a virtual shop front. It's a creative window into the soul of your business which reflects your brand values, beliefs and mission as well as allowing a unique insight into the person behind the business. It is a tool for your business. It is not your brand.

It's not CONTROLLED by the consumer - Although we take VAST amounts of time to discover who we are talking to and what they want, we only mould and evolve our offerings to present them in a consumer-friendly way. The values and beliefs behind your brand are unique to you and these are not influenced by the consumer. The offering, the way it is offered and the style it is offered in are variable factors. Consumers do not control the brand, they help to shape and evolve it.

So, now we are clear on what a brand is not. We can summarise all the above information to create the following statement about what a brand IS...

> **"A Brand is made up of a whole lot of building blocks forming a stable and consistent idea which, in turn, fills a consumer's needs, wants and desires."**

A brand is made up of:

The experience you provide: What do your clients FEEL from the service / product / culture you provide? What is the unique selling point of the feeling your customers get from what you offer?

The products and services you offer: What are the physical things you sell? What product or service have you created in order to give your target market the experience they want?

The promise you make for the experience you provide consistently: What are you offering, with certainty and consistency, for your customers to experience? What can you guarantee they will experience from your business EVERY SINGLE TIME they interact with you or use your product / service?

The culture you create for your tribe to be a part of, whether consumer or employees: How do you treat your employees and customers? What is the feeling they get when they interact with you? Do they feel part of a community or are they treated like royalty and well respected? What makes people WANT to work with you?

The values, beliefs and thoughts you have which created the idea - the core blocks: What are your own individual beliefs, values and thoughts that helped you create the idea for your business? **What is your businesses ethos,** your **values and beliefs?** What is your vision and your mission, both as an individual and as your business?

**BRAND IDENTITY = the visual elements
that make up your brand message**

Now we know that your brand image and the overall perception of your brand are so important, WHAT can you do to make sure this is always favourable for business?

Perception is the way in which something is regarded, understood, or interpreted. So HOW can you help the people your business is talking to have a POSITIVE and ACCURATE perception of you, your business and your brand?

Well... it all comes down to one super easy, super simple component:

CONSISTENCY.

This means consistency in EVERYTHING you do.

- EVERY touch point - every time you are seen, heard, felt and smelt!
- EVERY graphic
- EVERY Photo
- EVERY Message

- EVERY Caption
- EVERY Networking Event
- EVERY Video or Livestream
- EVERY Meeting, each time you answer the phone, or way you respond to an email.

> **MINDSHIFT - Every single time you represent your business or your business is being seen by anyone, BE CONSISTENT in everything you do.**

Now, this doesn't mean do the same thing every time. We know that we have to tweak and evolve our business and our message to tap into the right audience and connect with them.

What this does mean is that you have to ALWAYS REPRESENT your values, beliefs, thoughts, ethos, mission and vision. Always show up with the same EXPERIENCE and give the same FEELING to your onlookers. ALWAYS!

This means DON'T:

- Have a strong stance on an issue one day, then change your view completely and expect your audience to change with you the next.
- Use different colours and styling every time you are seen.
- Speak with a certain tone of voice, for example maybe down to earth and nurturing one day and then jump into serious, super official and stringent the next.

DON'T CREATE CONFUSION FROM INCONSISTENCY!

So, if you can help your onlookers create the right perception of your brand by BEING CONSISTENT in everything you do, WHAT does brand identity help you with? WHY DO YOU NEED TO CARE ABOUT IT?

Why branding is important for you

"Identity" is defined as the characteristics determining who or what a person or thing is. So here is the BIG juicy point!

You use your UNIQUE brand identity to showcase your brand.

You create exactly what you need to show your magnificence, your brilliance, your quirks, your personality and your level of fabulousness, and YOU USE IT TO SHOWCASE your AMAZING brand.

SIMPLE!

WHAT NOT TO DO

- Is to create brand identity from something you see on Pinterest or Instagram because you just love the colours and the look of it. Let's face it we are just going to be re-branding in six months using a method like this! it is a deeper creation process than this which is required to create your own unique brand identity - don't be tempted by quick ready-made schemes and palettes.
- Think that having a logo or colour palette means your brand identity is complete - it encompasses a WHOLE RANGE of factors, from your colours and logo to your message, your product and service, your packaging, the feeling you want to give your customers and so much more.
- Create a brand Identity that only YOU love. Your customers, target audience, perfect partner and whoever you are talking all need to be part of the creation process. You have to consider what they want from your brand; what they want to experience, feel, see, hear, touch and taste. Is the identity you are creating going to resonate and CONNECT with your dreamy soul mate?

SUMMARY:

CONSISTENTLY deliver and represent a brand identity that your customers want to experience, and you will **CREATE EMOTIONAL CONNECTIONS** that will get your target market returning, raving and gushing over you time and time again.

CHAPTER 5

POSITIONING

So now we're understanding a little more about why a brand is important for you, we can get a little deeper into the positioning of your brand, and what that means for your business.

As your brand is uniquely about you, first you have to be clear on exactly what it is going to stand for. Brand positioning is about being clear from the start as to:

- WHAT your brand is about
- WHO you are for
- WHY you are here, and
- WHERE you are unique

A good way to secure all of these different things is to set out your brand positioning statement. This statement is a short sentence or two, which sums up everything about your business. It doesn't need to be something you ever share with either your customers or in your marketing materials - it's more about getting clear in your own mind what you bring to the table.

When thinking about your brand positioning statement, you need to try and encapsulate all the important stuff you do, and stand for as a brand. Where are you different from your competitors? What makes your brand uniquely YOU? What does your brand FEEL like?

The best way to think about building a brand is to imagine you are creating a building. Your brand position needs to be the firm foundations of this building. Now, before you start any building, first you're going to consult an architect right? You're going to work out what shape the building is going to be. What size. What TYPE of building is it going to be? A house? A library? A shop? Each of these is going to need a different floorplan right? So you can't start to build until you're clear on this.

Once you've decided that you are building, let's say, a house, there's a whole load of other questions you need to be clear on again before your builder can start laying the bricks! How many people will live there? How many rooms do you need? What FOOTPRINT will the house have? Will you need to extend it after a few years? All of these details will be considered, and then the first job your builder will do, the very first thing to do is to lay the foundations IN THE RIGHT WAY.

It is exactly the same for your brand. If you can be clear at the start exactly what your brand is going to be, to stand for, who will be 'living' in what you will build, you will be securing the strong foundations in the right shape to easily accommodate the walls - the products, or services you're going to offer - and make sure it all works properly.

So try to think - what sums up your brand? What is the foundation, which is going to underpin everything you do and create?

Your brand values

Now you might hear people talking about their brand values from time to time, as they're also a vital part of LIVING your brand dream out in a way your dream customers can really CONNECT to.

Your brand values again might not ever be made explicit to your audience, but you need to be clear on WHAT they are, so that you can make sure that they are underpinning everything that you do.

You can start by listing out all the values, all the emotions which you want people to recognise where they interact with your brand. Write down as many as you can think of. What is going to be important to your audience? Maybe your wonderful brand is all about honesty. Or maybe your most important value is quality - making sure you deliver the best in everything you do. Your brand values list could contain words like trust, warmth, familiarity, or luxury, or fun, or excitement - the list really is limitless, but the important thing is to be real with yourself and your brand.

Once you have mapped out all these qualities, my advice would be to circle the three or four which speak most boldly to you. Anything more than five values to concentrate on is going to dilute your focus, but you want to be clear on a top tier of values which become your primary brand values. You can then refer back to these values time and time again, and make sure that every decision you take for your business is resonating with these principles.

Your brand values act as a map for guiding your brand in the right direction

Define your brand position visually

So, now you're hopefully getting clearer on WHAT your brand position and values is/are, you can start to think about what that means, visually, for your brand. Our visual experience is the primary way we experience the world, and so it's vital that you consider how your brand is going to LOOK.

Around 80% of what we learn about the world comes to us visually first, and yet many brand do not have a strong visual position that brings their written story to life. The words you will write will be important, as will the things you say, but before all of this, the thing which is really going to act like a MAGNET to your dream customer is HOW YOUR BRAND APPEARS.

So get clear, get intentional about how what visuals you are drawn to. What kinds of images are going to capture what you're all about? How are you going to tell your story and bring it to life for your audience with amazing visuals and images?

Think about your three key visual elements:

- Concept
- Visuals
- Colour

Each of these has a role to play when you're mapping out how your brand is going to appear in the world.

When we're talking about CONCEPT, we're thinking about the mood, the feeling, the overall EMOTION you want to trigger in your audience. The concept behind your imagery is so much more than just a location, or styling or the content of the images themselves. It's about trying to create something which is MORE than just the sum of its parts. It's a high-level FEELING that you want all of your imagery to share.

For the actual visuals themselves, when you're mapping out your positioning you might be thinking about things like the subject matter itself. Are you going to use lots of portrait shots? Or will it be more lifestyle photography. Does the viewer put themselves in the picture? How? How will your images look - sharp? Polished? Or soft and romantic?

Finally, we all know how important colour can be when used well to capture a mood or a feeling. Choose colours for you brand that you feel innately drawn to. You've got to LOVE what you create after all. If you're working with a designer, spend time learning from them about which colours work well for print, or online. Get exact about understanding precisely the universal reference numbers of the colours you choose for your brand, so you can be sure to be CONSISTENT in whatever you're creating. For print, you will need to know either the Pantone reference, or CMYK values for your chosen colour. For online, you'll need either the RGB or Hex reference numbers.

Make sure also that your images and shoots are going to complement your chosen brand colours too. We'll cover this in a little more detail later when we look at how to plan your brand shoot, but the key as ever is to completely UNDERSTAND the overall look and feel you are aiming for.

When you're clear about your brand position right from the start, everything else becomes 100% easier!

We're going to look in the next section at how some of the most successful women of our time have used and understood the power of branding to take themselves into the stratosphere. With a little bit of know-how - you can be next!

CHAPTER 6

BRAND CELEBRITY

Let's look more closely at some of the masters of branding - how they do what they do best, and what we can learn from their successes.

> **MINDSHIFT - YOUR BRAND CAN EASILY BE FAMOUS**

BRAND LIKE BEYONCÉ

A master brand builder, Beyoncé has skyrocketed her stardom by adopting some very simple steps in her brand building process. Aside from her huge and emotionally powerful talent, taking her brand from R&B to be a mainstream world renowned musical icon is a journey many other entertainers struggle and fail to accomplish all the time. So what is the key to Beyoncé's success? It can be summarised as the following:

Consistency

If there is one thing that Beyoncé shines bright on it is being consistently amazing. She shows up exactly as you would expect: sexy, unapologetic and whole heartedly woman! She roars into presence and that is how she ALWAYS represents herself. From the music she releases, to the outfits she wears, the performances she gives and the appearances she makes, Beyoncé is completely consistent representing her brand and we know, even though she may surprise and challenge the status quo, that whatever she does will be spectacularly sexy, empowering and the Beyoncé we have all come to know and love.

Habit Breaking

Beyoncé sets fire to a trend and sends it off in her own direction. Never one for going with the crowd, Beyoncé puts out albums and performances when it suits her. She gets people to look up and take notice by being innovative with her staging, her music and the medium she delivers her message through. Her visual albums and renowned eccentric staging were pioneering, and even though they opened her up to risk, the challenges paid off as she produced some of the most memorable works of the past two decades.

True and authentic to her brand promise

Allowing room for growth and evolution, going with the tides and the ebbs and flows of her industry, Beyoncé has kept her promise of openness and vulnerability whilst staying true to her mission of EMPOWERMENT of women through her journey.

Know your Tribe

Beyoncé knows she isn't for everyone. She knows her real, raw and authentic words and art, along with her provocative and sexy style, isn't going to tick the boxes for everyone. She doesn't try to be all things to all men. Beyoncé isn't about being EVERYTHING to EVERYONE. She is very aware of who makes up the 'Beyhive' of fans that follow her. She knows WHO her tribe is and she loves them hard. She shows up and gives them what they need and want, and doesn't even consider what those not in her tribe make of it!

Be Bold

Beyoncé is not known for her meek and mild persona or voice!! In her more recent works she literally sets fire to a house! She solidifies herself as a force to be reckoned with - do you think she took a moment to wonder 'Is this what everyone is going to like? Are people going to be pleased I am putting this record out?' Beyoncé is NOT afraid to have a strong impact and consistently show up for it! As we talked about in the last section, she knows who her tribe are and that she is a magnet to them for being IMPACTFUL and controversial. Beyoncé doesn't dull her sparkle - she keys up her own unique crazy and her tribe love her for it.

Beyoncé wasn't built in a day!

Collaborations, partnerships and getting raw and real have been the underpinning to Beyoncé's epic success and her longevity in the music industry. Yes, there is no denying her amazing talent and presence, but forming partnerships and collabs with other amazing artists have lifted her higher, inspiring and setting her alight, and helping her expose her full potential. By forming these incredible pairings, Beyoncé has showcased the best of herself, and stepped up to a level many can never reach.

Being real and raw is one of the most connecting ways Beyoncé has magnetized herself to her tribe. She doesn't care if people LIKE what she is saying, wearing, doing - she is being AUTHENTIC and telling her story HOW SHE WANTS people to see and hear it. If she makes a mistake or goes through something difficult she shares it, owns it and puts her mark on it and that is why her tribe love her.

BRAND LIKE OPRAH

Oprah is officially the BIGGEST one-woman brand in the world!

"A brand says, I can depend on you. I trust that what you have to offer is going to serve me well. I accept that. I'm a brand because I believe in the power of consistency." - Oprah Winfrey

Oprah has built her one of a kind, one-woman personal brands around being dependably genuine, and offering only what her tribe want and need. CONSISTENTLY. Building a brand like this is no mean feat, but ironically, can be accomplished by following a few very important ideals.

Oprah's personal stories

Lessons and life learning has helped Oprah not only relate to the people who are watching her shows, but by embracing the trauma and sadness of her early years she has created and cultivated an incredible emotional connection and bond of trust. Being authentic, transparent and vulnerable allows people to connect to you, and Oprah has truly used her personal experiences as an amazing tool for building a rock solid connection to her tribe.

Women Supporting Women

So, OK, Oprah hasn't just supported female lead business and professionals, she has a long and diverse list of brands and people she has openly and publicly supported. This allows her to create an even higher level of leadership, aspiration and credibility for herself, while showing she has a firm and strong opinion and voice which her tribe love her for.

She knows she is not a one-woman machine!

Oprah has openly shared the expert professionals she has curated to work alongside and around her. She knows where her strengths and expertise lie, and she has sought out the best of the best to do the work where she is weaker. This is one of the most important parts in building a strong and long lasting brand - define your strengths and weaknesses and get help on where you need the support to free you up to carry out the tasks, do the work and get on with the soul-aligned stuff that fires you up and showcases your brilliance!

Know your tribe and speak their language!

Oprah talks to her viewers, listeners and readers as if they are best friends popping in for a quick chat. When she gives an opinion, a view, or a referral for someone (or some thing) it is said with such authenticity that her tribe know she is saying it to help them. Keeping her language and her visual branding SIMPLE and clear, her tribe have easily been able to form a tight bond of trust. Oprah knows when something is AMAZING and the world needs telling. She hasn't just sat back and waited for a Facebook Ads expert to tell her how to showcase it, she has physically stood up and SHOUTED about it at the top of her voice. Oprah isn't afraid to AMPLIFY her message and create her own opportunities.

Personal Development

Oprah has always owned her mistakes, learnt from them and then come back stronger and more informed for making them! If you stumble or fall then OWN IT. Admit it, get up and keep going and make your brand about NOT RE-MAKING the same mistakes!

Oprah is OPRAH!

Being genuine and truly authentic is what skyrockets brands like Oprah and Beyoncé to stardom. They know what they have is GREAT, and they showcase it to their tribe in a way that there is no need for the BS to go on in the background. So, create products and services YOUR people want and need. And then be genuine and authentic in presenting them!

MINDSHIFT - IT IS NOT HARD TO BECOME A LEADER IN YOUR INDUSTRY

It's not hard to become a leading brand and it certainly does not have to take years to achieve! Whether you are starting out, building or renovating or simply refreshing your brand we need to address where you are and where you want to be.

It's important to gauge how well known your brand is to determine what stage you are currently at. Brand Celebrity is highly desirable. It is dreamed for, longed for, sought after by so many. And I'm here to show you how easily possible and achievable stepping into the celebrated limelight of brand extraordinary is for you, legacy building beauty!

CHAPTER 7

JADE'S STAGES OF BRAND CELEBRITY

Stage 1 - Idea / Concept / Start Up - Budding baby.

Do you have a fabulous idea and you just aren't sure what to do with it? Your brand is simply an idea or maybe you have just started the creation process. You have not been featured in any press or media articles or might just have had a brief review as a business idea to watch. You personally, legacy building lady, may have a following on social media or from a past business or endeavour, however this new brand is starting from scratch. You have few to no clients or customers, and your brand is not being talked about or recognised because it hasn't done the rounds required to gain visibility.... YET!

Stage 2 - You have been in business for a few years.

You had clients coming out of your one-man band ears and have been busy working and beavering away at producing / delivering the ACTUAL service or product your brand sells. You have tried several different looks for your logo and website colour scheme, and nothing seems to get your juices flowing. You don't have time to sit down and re-brand yet again just to change it all in a couple of months' time. You are caught between a rock and a hard place - not knowing where to turn to get this brand cemented in so you can up level the shit out of your biz.

Stage 3 - You have an established and recognisable brand.

You have a loyal customer base or returning and raving customers. You have grown and evolved, but your brand has stayed in a similar place. Now is the time you are aiming for the stars - you have big dreams and have figured out the magic way of incorporating a new branch-off under your existing brand but have no clue where to start. You know your existing branding needs a refresh / renovation to supercharge it into the new phase you're about to propel straight into.

Stage 4 - Darling, you were BORN to stand out!

Is your business instantly recognised where ever you show up? Do people immediately know the feeling your experience gives them the second your brand name is mentioned? Do people say you are a must have product or service? Are you featured EVERYWHERE and talked about all over social media as well as TV and press publications? Are you regularly included as a guest expert in your industry?

In summary, to get to grips with what level of BRAND CELEBRITY you are currently at answer these questions:

How to get everyone talking about your business:

- **Is your brand recognisable and often spoken about?**
- **Are you regularly featured in print, articles and expert spotlights?**
- **Have you made any famous alliances - affiliates or champions who have made your brand a must-have?**
- **Are you seen as an expert LEADER in your industry?**
- **Do you have a waiting list?**
- **Are you in more than one country?**
- **Do you have established and well followed (over 10,000 followers) social media accounts on multiple platforms?**

Want your brand to reach celebrity status?

BRAND EXTRAORDINARY

Reaching full on brand celebrity may not, in theory, be hard. Following a system of consistency, authenticity, connection, reliability, service and did I mention consistency really isn't all that difficult. But the reality of it is, not that many brands / businesses / amazing business people actually achieve it!! So really achieving the brand celebrity you have set out in your vision and your mission, is actually quite remarkable. And genuinely makes you and your business quite extraordinary.

Now we have figured out what level of brand celebrity you are currently in, and which one you WANT to be in, we need to spend a moment looking at what being an extraordinary brand means to you.

> **MINDSHIFT - "SUCCESS" COMES FROM HAVING CRYSTAL CLEAR VISION**

By having a vision that is so clear, so vivid and near on touchable in your imagination you can use this drive to achieve your version of "success". All you need to get there is:

    An Idea...

    A Plan...

    A Process...

    And some pure determination!!!

So knowing we need to outline this VISION in a crystal-clear manor, let's figure out what BRAND EXTRAORDINARY looks like for YOU.

Some questions for you to consider:

Are you striving to be a leader in your industry and market place? Are you wanting others in your industry to turn to you for mentorship and advice, to place you on a pedestal for the achievements you make in your speciality niche?

Do you want your tribe to see you as inspirational? Someone they can always rely on to inspire their thoughts ideas and beliefs into action? Someone they can turn to when they need to see clearly, and see a different way or path.

Are you looking for power? Do you want to the big word in your speciality? The buck stops with you and your opinion? Are your tribe looking for a final say in authority when they come to you and your brand?

Is setting the standards your bag? Do you love to be ahead of the game, creating the trends and designing innovative products and services that take people by surprise?

Can you see a different way for life? Is it your passion to instil a different, more fulfilled and life-living way to be?

Do you want your words to turn to £££? Do you want people to look to you to know what is hot and what is not? Are you looking to be seen and heard about what to buy and what to bin?

> **MINDSHIFT - YOU CAN GO FROM UNHEARD OF ONE MINUTE, TO IN THE NEXT BUILDING A LEGACY WORTH MILLIONS!**

Many people hide behind their brand whilst building it, perhaps avoiding the obvious hard work and soul-searching that needs to happen in order to create a STAND OUT brand. Don't wait and sit on your ideas because you think no one will notice, you can't be Beyoncé, you can't be Oprah you aren't Vogue! Wake up, get up stand up - your time is now!

STAND OUT

Leave your small thinking and long decision making at the door.

Now is YOUR TIME to dream big and then dream BIGGER!

Don't get left at the starting line in this fast paced and quick moving world - keep seeking out innovative ways to grow and evolve yourself and your business so that you my darling can...

STAND OUT from the crowd!

PART 3

WHAT IS THE PURPOSE OF YOUR SHOOT?

CHAPTER 8

WHAT ARE YOU SELLING?

Whether you are selling regularly updated products like seasonal fashion and accessories or offering a consistent selection of services, photography and videography will play a key role in the marketing and sales process.

When you think of items such related to fashion and accessories, the first thing that comes to mind is glossy magazine articles showing off the newest trends and must have items. Maybe also you might think of social media posts showing celebrities adorned in particular brands, or holding the newest designer items. This type of desire filled marketing isn't just for handbags and shoes.

Where service-based businesses go wrong with their marketing is that they do not have a vision for the same glossy, must-have type message around their offerings. They settle for out of date, usually non-professional snapshots of themselves and their products, and underestimate the huge and powerful value great photography and videography brings to the whole process.

So, now imagine for a moment that you a creating a campaign fit for Gucci, Versace, Jimmy Choo or Hermès when you are getting ready to launch your newest offering.

How would you approach your campaign knowing you are selling this iconic and premium class item?

How would you present yourself to the world knowing you have a beautiful piece of artwork launching for sale?

How would you contemplate showcasing your vision and stories around the creation of this beautiful offering to your audience?

MINDSHIFT - YOUR OFFERINGS ARE VOGUE WORTHY

YOU are Vogue worthy.

Now, Vogue may not be the 'be all and end all' for everyone. But for sure if you are not already showing up for your business and showcasing your offering in a Vogue-worthy way then you are not marketing to your full potential. You are not showing the respect and love to the offering you have created to help your dreamy client solve their biggest problem. You are not utilising all the avenues you have for showcasing your unique offering to the world.

Don't feel Vogue-worthy? Fake it till you make it! Do the work, be you and stand proud in that. No-one else has the unique set of characteristics and perceptions that you have. No-one else is the miracle that is you. No-one else can offer your unique perception around your offer, so stand strong and tall in knowing this and OWN it!

Put on your big girl pants and ask yourself how your audience want to feel when they see your offering showcased to the world. Do they want to feel underwhelmed and confused? Do they want to feel like they aren't sure who you are and what you are about? Do they want to feel like your offering is the same as a ton of others in your marketplace?

No.

They want to have their socks literally blown off!

They want you to make it SO EASY for them to emotionally connect to your brand, to fall in love with you and the experience you are promising them, to UNDERSTAND AND BUY your offering that is going to solve their problem and help them find happiness!!

Ever wondered why you pick up the glossy mags, be it health related, hobby related, home and garden related, fashion related, women and baby or any of the others you might feel drawn to? WHY do you pick them up? And WHY do you love them?

Because they make you feel excited. They help you find answers for your problems by SHOWCASING products and services and information in a glossy, clear and easy to understand way! They emotionally connect with you on every level. They tick all your boxes and they make you FEEL thrilled to read them!

So why have you not done this for your own offering? For your own business which you have given every single moment of your being to. You have sweated and worked and grown and evolved, and then worked some more to create this business that provides a solution and solves problems, enabling people to get closer to happiness and feel thrilled! Why do you not value showcasing this to the highest level as your top marketing tool?

Your dreamy client wants you and your brand to show up exactly how they need you and when they need you, offering them the solution to their biggest worry, concern and trouble, in a way that they can immediately get a sense of the thrill you are going to give them when their problem has been solved.

So, what are you selling?

> Is it a product?
>
> Is it a service?

Are you regularly relaunching the same thing or are you seasonally changing your items?

Are you launching a one-time offer, like an event or a retreat?

Make some notes on what you are planning in the next twelve months - maybe you are launching a new website or revamping an existing one. Maybe you are planning on launching a refreshed social media content strategy, or tapping into a new platform. Maybe you are going to be having printed marketing material made for trade shows or events.

Now, physically write down the products and services you are launching or planning to launch in the next 12 months. Write down whether these items are going to be re-launched in the future or whether they are replaced seasonally etc. Are they regularly offered for example 1-2-1 coaching or consulting?

Now take some time to brainstorm the stories that have helped create your business and the stories that have inspired the creation of the product or service you have brought to life.

Finally think about WHERE you are going to be offering these products and services.

What do the touch points look like? For example - you could be having social media cards made with an opt in, leading to a landing page, leading to a download, opting in to an email sequence. Write down all the touch point chains that your different products and services have.

Establishing exactly what products and services you are currently selling, and what you are planning to sell throughout the next twelve or so months will give you a great idea as to how many campaigns you will need to create. This in turn will inform where you will be able to utilise photography and film in your marketing.

CHAPTER 9

WHO IS YOUR CLIENT?

The first step to establishing the purpose of your shoot is to figure out WHAT you are selling. Now we have made notes around this, we can move to on the MOST important question which is:

WHO IS YOUR CLIENT?

In the branding section of this book, we covered the importance of creating your dreamy client avatar. We are going to look at HOW you create this, and how you then use this information to market to them easily, engagingly and authentically.

As we covered earlier, YOUR CUSTOMERS DON'T BUY YOU - THEY BUY THEIR HIGHEST VALUE. So how exactly do you understand and get clear on what their highest value is?

You have to first establish WHO it is you are wanting to get clear on. The list below contains the types of questions we can ask ourselves when we're trying to identify who our dream client it. The list is extensive however these are not the ONLY questions you can ask. Feel free to add more on, to elaborate on others - do whatever feels most organic and aligned with you. Don't forget also that some of these questions may not be relevant to your industry and there may be others you feel are more relevant.

Please take these as a guideline, add change and tweak them as necessary.

To begin, I want you to imagine you are thinking of just one dream person.

So who is your dreamiest client?

Who is it that has the problem that you offer the unique solution to?

Here is a huge list of questions you can ask yourself, that I have used with women in various professions. Some will be relevant, some not so much. Use these as a starting point and tweak, evolve, remove, replace and add to as necessary:

How old are they?

Are they male or female?

Where in the world do they live?

What does their home look like?

Do they have a family?

Do they have a large circle of friends and acquaintances?

Are they motivated by money? Do they save a lot of money? Do they spend a lot of money?

Are they high earners? Are they low earners?

Are they hard workers?

What career do they have? What industry is it in?

What characteristics do they have?

What do they do in their free time?

Who do they spend their free time with?

What matters to them?

Where do they shop?

Why do they shop there?

How do they shop? Online, chain stores, boutiques, ethically?

How were they educated?

What do they read?

What do they watch?

Do they have their hair professionally cut? Go to a barber or a salon?

Do they DIY their hair?

Do they spend money on having day spa experiences? Track days? Manicures and pedicures?

Are they an animal person? Do they prefer dogs or cats or both? Do they love horses? Do they keep horses? Do they have hobbies that involve animals?

Are they married?

Are they divorced?

Are they widowed?

Have they had health problems?

Do they worry about their health?

Do they go to the gym?

Do they have a certain diet they follow i.e vegan

Are they members of any clubs?

Do they have disposable income?

Are they a saver or a spender?

Do they have children?

Do they have grandchildren?

Do they have siblings?

Are their parents alive?

Do they spend time with their parents / siblings?

Have they struggled to have children?

Are their children IVF or natural?

Why do they live where they live?

Do they drive?

What do they drive?

Why did they choose that brand?

Are they religious?

Are they political?

What books do they love?

What films do they love?

What celebrities do they admire?

Who do they look up to?

Who are their idols?

Who do they follow on social media?

What social media do they use?

Do they have a smartphone?

What brand is it?

Where do they go on holiday?

How often do they go on holiday?

Why do they go that often and to that destination?

Who do they holiday with?

Why do they get out of bed each day?

When you have answered a lot (if not al!) of these questions, you have a much clearer idea of WHO you are serving. We then need to establish WHAT their problem is, to make sure your offering is aligned with their needs.

What problems does this person have?

- Brainstorm at least 10 problems they have.
- Which of your products and services offer them help with their problem?

Have you identified any gaps that your current offerings have for solving your dreamiest of dream clients' problems? GREAT!! Use your notes to fill the gaps with ideas that you can use to evolve and tweak your offering to fulfil their needs.

Now, list out what the MOST IMPORTANT problem you solve is. You are now well on your way to stepping up your offering to the next level!

CHAPTER 10

HOW DOES IT LOOK RIGHT NOW?

We have figured out WHAT you are selling and WHO you are selling to. Let's take some time to evaluate how that offering looks right now.

Work through these questions, noting down your answers:

- What are you currently offering?
- HOW are you currently offering it?
- How are your clients finding out about your offering?
- DO you have sales pages / landing pages and opt ins?
- Do you have physical printed marketing materials leaflets flyers etc.?
- Are you using social media to promote the product or service?

By establishing what you are doing right now to promote your offering, we can narrow down what is working and what needs improvement.

Here's a few more for you - by answering the following questions we can gauge the level promotion you have currently got going and how it is working for you. Think:

Do you sell online only?

Do you have social media campaigns around specific offerings?

Do you have a call to action on every social media post, and if so is your click to call to action more than 15% conversion?

Do you have landing pages for each of your offerings with specific call to actions and touch point chains following them up?

Do you have a regularly growing following on social media?

Do you advertise your offering anywhere?

Are you being regularly featured in print and guest expert articles showing up for your offering?

Do you have a brand website?

When you offering your product / service are you telling the story of WHY it exists?

Are you showing your potential customers the PROBLEM it solves and how it is going to make them feel?

It's so crucial in building your brand to be honest, and see clearly what you have, what is working, and where there is room to build. You are in absolutely the BEST position to transform your brand to the next level of success, so take the time to truly understand your offering first. Once you're clear on this, you are well on your way to STANDING OUT!

CHAPTER 11

STEP OUT OF YOUR BOX

Ok, so we have established:

> What you are selling.
>
> Who you are selling it to.
>
> And what is working / not working for your campaigns right now.

So this is the time that we need to look at how you present it.

Now it's ok to think that you can "get away" with a few shots of your product, or your course, or a nice stock image of something relating to the concept of your offering. For example, if you're a life coach, this could be something like a lovely horizon with the sun rising looking inspirational. However in order to uplevel your business and form the strong immediate emotional connection with your audience we are after, you need to use images that show them how it FEELS.

> How it feels to WORK with you...
>
> How it feels to have the results you deliver...
>
> How it feels to use your product...
>
> How it feels once you have used your product...

This is the key to forming that strong connection with your client right from the start. Now I want to explain exactly how you need to do this. So let's imagine you are looking at going on a holiday. What is the first thing you do?

Do you have a look on the internet at the destination you are considering?

Do you pick up the glossy holiday mags and flick through the offering of countries and resorts?

Do you have a go-to travel agent who you send your request to, who will send you back some details?

Either way you are going to be looking for the VISUALS! You are going to be looking for the pleasure from your holiday. Now it's true that sometimes the flight time may be a factor in your decision making process BUT if you want something that you can only specifically get in a country that is a 14 hour flight away, then you are going to endure that 14 hour flight to get there!

So, let's suppose you have the brochure or the online pages for the resorts you're considering. What are you looking for from this information? You are looking for the dramatic and impressive entrance - the hotel grounds, swimming pools, breathtaking views and scenery. You are looking for the details of the activities and facilities on the site and you want to know what the food and dining experience is like. You are wanting to see the room and the views from the room, you want to know the bed and the bathroom are acceptable to your expectation.

And how does the resort communicate this to you?

They have a lovely write up and descriptions around all of these factors, but really is that the first thing you do - read the copy?

No.

You look at the images.

You want to see a magnificent video showing you other people just like you , at that destination, enjoying the resort. You want to see images of the amazing food and drink, plus the entertainment experience, capturing the expressions of those enjoying and relaxing.

You want to hear and see the ripples of the swimming pool, and imagine yourself there, relaxing. If it is a family holiday you're planning, you want to see children being accepted and accommodated, while parents are safe in the knowledge they can relax and enjoy watching their children having a fabulous time. You want to smell and taste the food as it is freshly cooked, and you want to feel like you are sitting with the other guests who are already there enjoying the holiday you are desiring.

You want to know about the local area, you want to see the locals and feel their culture and their passion for the area they live in. You want to feel part of the community knowing your holiday is going to provide you the experience you are yearning for.

The resort does this with video and images!

Video and images tell all these stories.

They suggest all these feelings and experiences, and they give you a VISUAL insight into them being a reality. They allow you to transport yourself to the resort before you have ever physically been there. They give you the chance to feel, smell, touch and taste everything as if you are a returning loyal customer.

So now consider the feelings and experiences you NEED to showcase in order to sell your offering to its highest potential. You need to think outside the box of showing a quick glimpse of the actual physical product, and instead start telling its full and detailed story.

Start sharing what it feels like to have this product in your life offering you the solution to the problem that is causing you pain.

Start sharing what it feels like to work with you! And what it feels like when you have worked with you!

You need to step up! And be seen. You need to get on camera for photography and videos that tell YOUR story and why you are the expert in providing this unique solution your dreamy clients NEED and WANT right now.

You need to create emotional connections to EVERY AREA of your brand.

You need to evoke all of the senses in your target audience and help them EASILY make the buying decision, by giving them the answer to all their questions, by showing them the feelings they are going to have from your experience and ticking all of their boxes visually before they even have to read the copy.

So, in summary:

Step up - Get in front of the camera and tell your story for EVERY CAMPAIGN.

Be seen and heard - Use video to convey your unique message and why you are an expert in solving your dream clients problems.

Use graphics and stock images - Support your photography and videography with CUSTOM MADE stock images that give life to your message, and offer the support your campaigns need in a consistent and recognisable way.

PART 4

INTRODUCTION TO PHOTOGRAPHY

CHAPTER 12

THINKING ABOUT PHOTOGRAPHY

Throughout history, images have played a vital part in our shared experience. The human mind is primed to remember what it can SEE. Even thousands of years ago, people were creating simple images on cave walls to represent the world around them - simple stick figures, animals, handprints. We've come a long way since then, but our shared human experience of creating, and appreciating beauty represented visually has not changed. From the old masters like Leonardo Da Vinci, through to today's in-demand high fashion photographers like Mario Testino and Annie Leibowitz, the evolution of imagery and how we use it has been so important to our societies.

When we're thinking about BRANDS, it's photography and the use of images which have really been the most powerful driving force in bringing brands to life. If we try to think of brand campaigns which have been memorable for us over the years, it's the IMAGES which come to mind first - think of the Guinness adverts, with their moody, swirling atmospheric imagery, or the iconic Wonderbra shot from the 'Hello Boys' campaign. Images can become instantly iconic, as great photography is such an immediate route to our emotions, desires and passions.

The images you use when you are building your brand from the ground up are SO important. With your photography, you set out your stall, SHOWING not telling your ideal customer exactly:

Who you are

What you are all about, and

HOW you will make them feel.

Your brand has to encapsulate ALL of this, and sometimes you will only have a split second to communicate all this! Your images are the route to creating those instant connections with your customers.

Your brand is so much more than just a colour palette and a logo. It's the way in which you fulfil your promises to your customers - the imagery you use throughout EVERY touchpoint in their journey getting to know you is the basis of this emotional connection.

Think about it - we can probably all picture in our minds eye a time when you've seen an image, whether it's in a magazine, or online somewhere, that has really spoken to you. It's grabbed you, made you stop what you were thinking about, and prompted you to turn your full attention to it. Maybe it was a beautifully shot ad in a glossy magazine for a perfume. Something about the colours, the tones, the styling of the image made you think - "I WANT whatever this is!" before you even realise it is an advert.

Or maybe simply the headline image when you click through to a new site speaks to you, and you instantly feel that "YES! This brand KNOWS who I am already".

It's this power that with the right help you can learn to harness, to build your brand a solid foundation that INSTANTLY connects with your dreamy client. There are a couple of things to keep in mind as you start to think about how to make photography work for you and your brand. So let's take a look!

Making photography work FOR YOU

The photography you use has to really capture the essence of everything your brand is. In the early stages, it can be tempting to try and short cut the thinking behind this. I see a lot of people who fall back on familiar kinds of images which, whilst they are very beautiful, don't actually tell any kind of story about WHO they are.

Try to keep the EXPERIENCE your brand will create at the front of your mind when using photography. Is that experience which is shown in your potential shot, really telling your audience anything about how you are going to make them feel? About your core brand values? For example, if you are a coach, you might be drawn to an image of a hand creating a 'heart' shape with the fingers to represent the care you dedicate to your clients, but is this really going to have an emotional IMPACT for them? Or would a vibrant image of a successful woman living her best life speak more immediately to WHERE you will end up taking THEM, as a result of that care? It is down to you to make sure you're crafting the right story for your brand, and then bringing it to life through your images.

Be mindful about choosing RELEVANT images for the emotions and feelings you want your audience to feel. Just because you work daily on a laptop, does that mean you have to use this in an image because everyone else in your sector is? NO! Maybe for your dream audience, a better way to showcase what you do is to look at images which will transport THEM to where they want to be in life!

What is the photographic style of your brand?

Let's think back for a second to that glossy perfume ad we just talked about. Perhaps it's a Chanel advert for a classic fragrance. You can guarantee that every single thing about the shot on that glossy magazine page has been thought about in MINUTE detail, from the composition, to the colours, to the model, to the styling, to the accessories, to the makeup, to the lighting, to the pose.... The list is endless. Thousands of hours of preparation will have gone into creating that one, single image.

Why?

Because a global powerhouse brand like Chanel know EXACTLY who they are. They understand the VALUE that their images have. They know PRECISELY how to create the emotional connection they are looking for with their audience. They know that in a single second, that image will speak to YOU, and spark your interest. They also understand how that one, single image makes sense in the context of all the other single images and campaigns they have ever run.

The success of that one campaign image in stopping you in your tracks comes because it is part of the bigger brand story. It perfectly captures on its own everything you need to know about WHO the Chanel woman is, but it also is part of their ongoing brand story.

So what does this mean for us, as legacy brand building ladies? How can we identify and start to build this kind of incredible brand consistency in our images?

The trick is to identify where and how you can be consistent in your images. We're all familiar with the idea of Instagram filters, and how you can use them to build a consistent look and feel. So think about the overall style of your brand, and what this could look like for you. We need to make sure that those styles - whether it's the colours in your logo, or the tone of voice you use in your writing comes across visually too.

If your brand is aimed at a young, fun, millennial audience, think what types of image are going to resonate with them best? Maybe it's punchy, bold images. Or maybe your images have a quirky, retro vibe?

What your audience will want to see if they look at a feed of your images, is that they can understand at a glance what you're all about. If all your posts contain gorgeous pastel tones, and soft gold-hued images, it is going to jar a little if in the middle of all that you have a heavy, dark moody shot with a completely different image style. By thinking about these sorts of questions BEFORE you start communicating with your dreamy client, you can build this brilliant brand consistency right from the start.

Your audience want to be EXCITED when they look at your images. They WANT you to deliver for them, to make them FEEL engaged with you or your products, and they want you to draw them in so they can lose themselves in the excitement of discovering how you'll meet their needs. If you can deliver this kind of consistency in the style of your photography, you'll be on the way to a beautifully curated brand feed which sets your customers interest alight!

What about typography and images?

Now there will be times when you want to be able to use words as well as images. Even our perfume advert will likely have the name of the product as well as the brand as a minimum. Creating your imagery extends to the way you treat your type, when creating assets for you brand.

Think about the size, colour and FEEL of the fonts you choose. The same image could conjure up two very different feelings if the messaging over it is in a flowing, freeform script instead of a clean, blocky font. Your fonts are every bit a constituent part of your brand, and it pays to think about how you can make them work with your images at the outset.

I see lots of people who have a great idea for the style of images they want to put out around their brand. They have a great social media plan, and the images are stunning, but all are let down because the COLOUR of the font they've chosen doesn't show up well against the images the use it on. If you have a very detailed shot, with lots of patterns, textures and different colours, it can be very tricky to find space to overlay a message on the top without patches of the writing getting 'lost' against the detail. So think about HOW you're going to use your images, and if you are going to need to overlay any other content on top of them.

The same goes for web images. Will you need to overlay your logo over the top of a hero banner image on your website? If so, you're going to need to make sure there is 'clean' space within your image at the right points so your logo is not competing with the background for attention!

When and where should photos be used within your brand?

The short answer is that there are a LOT more places you're going to need great images than you probably realise when you're just starting out! If we start from the very basics, you might be thinking about needing a headshot, so your audience can SEE who you are. But think - once you have this, WHERE are you going to put it? On your website? Of course you are. But then how many OTHER pages are there on your site which are also going to need some great shots? And how often are you going to need to refresh your website, to keep things fresh?

We all know by now that an online presence is SO much more than just a website. How many social platforms are you active on? What about content for each of them? How does your audience across the various social media sites differ? Are they coming to you for different parts of your offering on Facebook to how people engage with you on Twitter? If so, you're going to want to tailor your content specifically for these people, which is likely to mean a different suite of images for both.

Then there's also all the more 'traditional' offline ways you can communicate your lovely brand to the people you need to reach.

Maybe you take part in lots of events, in which case you might need to think about what printed materials you can physically GIVE to your ideal customer. Take it from me that if you try to print out low res shaky screenshots you've grabbed online, your clients are going to notice, and NOT for the right reasons!

SUMMARY

So, feeling ready to dive into the world of photography?! Here's a quick checklist to make sure you're covering the basics in your planning:

- SHOW your customer who you are
- Build EMOTIONAL connection through your images
- Think as your customer does, and create for THEM
- Be relevant
- Map out your image STYLE - are you bright? High contrast? Saturated?
- Think about image treatments - will you use full bleed images, or borders? What type?
- Be consistent
- Plan for different image uses
- Most importantly, EXCITE your audience. Draw them in. Ask questions. Grab their attention with your images and DO NOT LET GO!

In the next section, we're going to look in a bit more detail about connection, and how we can use imagery to set off that spark.

CHAPTER 13

CONNECTION

"We empower them, we ignite them, we set them alight in our hearts and minds."

"It's not about YOU, it's about what you do for them."

Early on in my business journey, this had been the most poignant marketing advice I had heard. And it is so true. It is all about the problem you can solve, the experience you can give, the feeling you can make someone feel. All of the marketing courses, experts and coaches I worked with and invested into have believed this same statement and come from this same position. And it's right.

To a point.

What I have found, is this: In order to get people to engage with you so you can SHARE the miraculous, life changing impactful service or products you have created for them, they have to want to LISTEN to you. They have to want to hear you, see you, know you.

In order to create the trust they NEED, to be able to buy from you, they have to WANT to have this relationship with you.

And this is where it becomes about you.

This is where in under six seconds you need to tell your story so strongly, authentically and relatably that your audience WANT to connect with you. So that they want to form this emotional bond, this powerful connection with you, so that they are then OPEN to hearing, seeing, experiencing all you have to offer. In short, cultivating the stepping stones to a lasting relationship with you.

I put this question out in a couple of communities I am a part of a while ago and the response I received to this was really varied:

"What does creating emotional connection mean to you and why do you feel it's important?"

Take a look at a few of the responses:

"Emotional connections happen through true authenticity and cannot be faked. If you try to be somebody you are not, people will see right through the lies and you lose credibility.

As a coach, it is crucial for me to have an emotional connection with my clients. If we don't vibe, the coaching really doesn't flow as it should and amazing results are difficult to achieve."

"You can't really create an emotional connection. It's either there or it's not. You can cultivate one, growing it from something small, just like you would in any relationship (familial, friend, romantic) - but you can't 'pouf' one into existence. (Why some dates will never turn into relationship and some people would never be an ideal client). For me, it's important to connect with people with whom there IS an emotional connection NATURALLY. It feels best and allows more growth and meaning. I do believe that when we SHOW UP as ourselves, emotionally physically spiritually mentally, then it lets other people connect with us and vice versa. So really, the more emotionally connected we are ourselves, and are out in the world as ourselves, the more connected we'll feel to others. Connection is like an open door to possibility."

"It's incredibly important, to the point I could ramble off on a long-ass tangent - but I won't. In short: a brand must have a personality in order for a consumer to have a relationship with it. Therefore, you NEED a personality to create a connection that ultimately cultivates a relationship. Skip this, and you're doomed. (Disclaimer: unless you're a 'meets a need' business i.e. plumber, tow truck, electrician etc.)"

From these reactions we can summarise the importance that comes in HAVING emotional connection. But there is debatability around whether emotional connections are "created".

Now for me, this is the point of view I am coming from, this is what I wholeheartedly believe.

I feel that you CAN create an emotional connection.

You can choose TO create it or NOT to create it. But either way there is a definite argument for the creation factor around connections. A connection isn't something that exists without reason. There is ALWAYS a reason the emotional connection or connection of any kind with another human being, object or thing(!) exists. And this is why I think that...

Imagine for a moment, you're standing in line in a coffee shop. Loads of others in front and behind you. You look to the counter and see three people serving. Now, one of them is an normal looking, young girl and she's moving quickly to get through the orders. Another is an older lady and she is on the till chatting and engaging with customers. And the third is a young lad who is struggling to keep up with the other workers and looks highly under pressure.

Ultimately you are going to make a decision over which one of these workers you WANT to serve you your drink.

This decision is going to be made from a variety of different places, some that we don't want to acknowledge that we go to - like judgement, for example. We are going to make a quick judgement of the three workers over their ability to fulfil our highest VALUE. And it is this highest value that is going to be the KEY FACTOR in creating the emotional connection that is going to see you choose the worker you feel best suited to serve your drink.

Now, if you value efficiency over interaction then you are probably going to determine that the young girl is going to be your best hope of a speedy and precise cup of joe. If you crave interaction and friendliness than the older lady is going to float your boat and do the best job in your eyes. However, if you feel empathy, if you feel underdog syndrome and give everyone a chance you are automatically going to be drawn to the young boy who is trying hard, and struggling to keep up. He is going to be your ideal coffee server today.

Now, I'm not going to get super deep into the WHY around these values you have. I simply want you to see that emotional connections, and connections of any kind, can be created from the smallest glimpse of someone or something. A tiny amount of information then creates a perception, an idea, a suggestion around WHO someone is, or what something is. Which, in turn, ticks a box for you as the decision maker, and allows them or it to connect to you, therefore giving them more time, more attention, and overall a chance to impact on your life.

Take our coffee shop scenario again for a moment. Now you have decided the young girl who is cracking on through the orders, is going to be the one to serve you your beloved first cup of coffee of the day, because efficiency is what you are all about. You have also decided there is no way you are going to have the older lady because she is delaying the queue by chatting unnecessarily, and the young boy is just a disaster - he is more likely to spill your drink all over you than serve it to you. Now as you get closer to the counter you make a split second eye contact with the young girl who you feel looks annoyed to see you. She looks at you like she doesn't want to serve you your coffee, you are adding to her list and she is about had enough.

What do you think happens in this moment?

The connection you made to this person is at an immediate disconnect. You are offended that she has given you this look and you immediately choose the older lady as the ideal candidate to serve you your drink. You think 'she is friendly after all, at least I will get coffee and a smile to start my day'.

Now what has happened here?

You have created a disconnect towards the young girl, whose mind you can apparently read and created a CONNECTION with the older lady who is now your only hope of a cup of coffee this morning.

Can you see how easily connections are to make and to break? Can you see how split seconds decision can impact hugely on the connection you choose to make with someone or something?

Now, when you get to the counter, it is actually the young boy you get to serve you your drink. And he does it quickly, and without incident. And you feel so pleased for him that he did a great job that you take note of his name and you tip him and wish him a great day. Then you leave thinking about the great cup of coffee and lovely young man who served it to you.

A connection has been formed.

A connection you didn't think you wanted to form.

A connection you didn't expect to make.

And in fact, that young man who did a good job is who you now always remember and think of when you go back to that coffee shop.

Connections can be CREATED, and they can occur at ANY POINT of relationship or journey.

If you can form the connection...

>...By being the business your dream clients WANT to serve them.

>...By giving the experience at EVERY TOUCH POINT of communication that your dream client WANTS TO HAVE, and

>...By providing the product and service, giving them the ultimate feeling that they WANT TO EXPERIENCE...

...Your connection will be solidified as a strong emotional bond. And you will have another raving fan to add to your business.

SUMMARY

So, in knowing that CONNECTION CAN BE CREATED at any point of your business journey, how are you showing up to allow your target audience to create this connection with you? Are you giving them a vast amount of opportunities to connect to you? Are you showing them an abundance of suggestions of you and your story?

This is where storytelling, and doing it over and over and suggesting, and glimpsing and getting real is going to set your business alight.

CHAPTER 14

PHOTOGRAPHY AND STORYTELLING

> **MINDSHIFT - Nothing is more powerful than a story**

Photography gives an INSIGHT into the story you want to tell. Photography gives a suggestion of the story without telling the full thing. It is the most powerful tool to draw people in, to connect with them, to create a reality where everything is exactly as it needs to be.

You might have heard talk about 'storytelling' in the world of brands. In a world where we're constantly bombarded with information, how can we cut through the noise and help our dream clients UNDERSTAND the value of our wonderful brand? We do this by creating STORIES. We build a narrative which takes the customer on a journey. Makes them ask questions. Gives them a FEELING they love, and want to share.

Think about a story you know well, perhaps off by heart. You can remember every detail about what happens, who the characters are, WHY they are making the choices they do, and you get that insight from a story into how they are actually FEELING.

This is what you need to create for your own audience

The human brain can remember lots of facts, but it's the ones which are woven into STORIES which stay with us the longest.

Whether you read it in a book and conjure in your mind how the characters look, or immerse yourself in a beautifully shot film, a story can transport you immediately to another emotional place. They give you a FEELING. Through a narrative, we really connect with what the author or director wants us to know, and wants us to experience.

I'm going to show you how great photography is the cornerstone for building your own brand story.

> **MINDSHIFT - Photography used in Business NEEDS to be used as a project series to tell the WHOLE AND FULL story**

One head shot gives a suggestion of who you are. One head shot gives the IDEA of who you are, but it is a slim and small amount of information. Once you get on board and embrace the reality that your brand NEEDS to tell your dream customer the STORY they are looking for, you'll begin to see how photography can really open this up, and create a world of possibilities.

Your images are the very first part of your brand story. We've already touched on how important visual language is. Our eyes are drawn to beauty, and beautiful images FIRST, before we notice any of the other detail which might surround them. Think back to our travel brochure analogy - flicking through, the things which get you really excited about potential destinations to visit are...the IMAGES! Yes, the detail is important, yes you might need to check the price, but your heart will almost always be captured by a great photograph FIRST, before any of the other factors come into play.

For your brand, the images will often be the first touchpoint your potential customers have when they come across your offering. On some social platforms, you don't even get the opportunity to explain in words about who you are, or what your brand is all about until you've reached that point of STOPPING someone in their tracks with an image. It's your visuals which will get them to stop. It's the photographs which will finally have them asking the right questions and clicking to find out more.

Your images have the power to start that conversation.

SO imagine you are actually sitting with a friend, telling them a story. You're having a conversation. Now depending on a number of factors - how much time you have, how well you know that person, what sort of mood they are in - will determine the way you tell your story.

Maybe you know that time is short, so you'll tell the entire story in one go. Or maybe you know they're already interested in hearing what you have to say, so you can take your time a little, elaborate on the details. Perhaps throw in a few jokes, or ask what they think.

The principle is EXACTLY the same when thinking about your brand and your photography. Sometimes, you'll need to use a powerful image which tells you entire brand story, even if it was to stand alone. Your image needs to communicate all the important things in an instant about who your brand is, how you can meet your audience WHERE THEY ARE, and WHERE your brand will take them.

Then, there will be other times where your images will need to work as part of a bigger picture. When the story itself becomes the sum of lots of parts. When you treat your images as part of a SERIES, building the story and narrative as you go. The more your client sees, the more their understanding and emotional response to your brand will grow too.

So don't forget:

- Your brand tells a story
- Your images start that conversation
- Your photography is the MOST POWERFUL way to build the connections you need with your desired audience

What is the narrative you are looking to tell?

From portraits to lifestyle work, narratives play a HUGE part in telling the story of your brand. If you were to caption the message you want to get across to your audience with words what would they say?

For example:

> "I bring fun, enthusiasm and energy to all my projects."

How would you visually represent this statement? Would the scene be dark, moody and dramatic, full of silence and stillness?

OR

Would you use colour and movement to create excitement, happy expressions and uplifting backgrounds?

> "The feeling of luxury oozes from every part of my business and service."

Would this visually be represented with a rustic, down to earth coffee shop and you looking hard at work?

OR

Would you choose a high end restaurant, showing the laughter and approachability you bring to client meetings, while maintaining the high expectation of clients being well looked after?

Let's try one more.

> "I am a professional. I bring knowledge, experience and a kind and warm experience free from judgement."

What would you expect from a headshot of someone with this bio? Would you expect them to be sipping a margarita on a beach somewhere?

OR

Would you expect them to be open, with a smiling friendly appearance, clean, crisp and smartly dressed?

The narrative is the most important part for telling your story. This needs to be represented authentically in BOTH visuals and written copy.

Telling visually appealing stories

We know that photographs prompt questions. And when your audience are asking questions, that's when we know we have truly captured their interest.

With beautiful photography, you can create mystery, create drama, create intrigue. You can draw people in to your images, by sweeping them away into an image which prompts them to feel an instant emotional connection. Think of the types of image you are naturally drawn to. There will be a certain something which resonates for you, which exactly meets your need at that time, and prompts you to want to find out more about that image.

With a great visual narrative, the viewer will find themselves wondering HOW the emotion they are feeling came to be.

So let's try something. Think of an image from your past which really spoke to you. Perhaps it was a page from a fashion magazine you used to have pinned on your wall. Or maybe an image of a destination you loved, which you dreamed of constantly. Or a still from a film where you longed to experience the same life some day.

Can you identify the EMOTIONS these images brought out in you at the time? What was it about them which captured your attention? Try to list out in your mind the words which that picture made you feel about the person you wanted to be:

Fearless? Brave? Confident? Adventurous? Free?

Beautiful? Content? Loved? Strong?

Now think back to what else was taking place in your life during the time that image became important to you. The chances are that the emotions you've just listed FIT into the overall narrative of your life story at that time.

> **The image called to you because it MET YOUR EMOTIONAL NEED.**

Your brand can create these same experiences for your dreamy customers, when you understand the story your images are telling, and what that will mean. You can build a powerful relationship and draw people in before you have said a single word.

CHAPTER 15

WHAT IF YOU DIDN'T USE IMAGES?

Imagine a world without pictures. Pretty dull right?!

The importance of using great photography and great visuals for you brand is about so much more than being 'interesting'. It's about capturing people's attention in a moment.

> Did you know you have approximately **six seconds** to make an impact?

Your audience will make snap judgements constantly on where to spend their attention. We're surrounded by images now, in every medium. In a world where everyone is competing for attention you have to make sure that you're keeping up in order not to get lost.

Our brains are AMAZING!

The human brain processes images around **sixty thousand times faster** than words. Sixty THOUSAND. If you think about it, over 90% of human communication is visual. Those words someone is saying? Whilst you are listening to them, you're also WATCHING their body language to try and pick up on how they are feeling. You're monitoring their lips, so your brain can reinforce the sound they're making and truly hear the words. You'll be checking their expression for clues as to the right response - should you be smiling? Commiserating? Outraged?

Most of our understanding comes from what we SEE, whether we realise it or not. We all have a gut instinct, and innate 'sixth sense' when something is just not right, and often this will have been brought about by the subtle visual cues we pick up on without even realised we're doing it.

You simply CANNOT ignore the importance of visual communication when you're building your brand. The world is constantly changing, and as technology evolves, so does the ability to communicate visually. Think how drastically the world has changed even since the invention of the smartphone. We are now served images and video on the go, all the time from so many different sources - from friends, from brands, from the news - which in the past we would have had to deliberately seek out. We are bombarded with images and content now, and it is up to US as consumers to CHOOSE how to respond to them.

This visual information is instant in a way that traditional written ways of communicating are not. In a split second, your audience will have made a judgement on whether or not to pay attention to your brand and your story. So it's no surprise that articles with images can get up to a 94% increase in views than ones without.

Why WOULDN'T you want to tap into this?

You need to make it EASY for your dream customers to find you. Easy for them to understand your offering. You need to make it so simple for them to WANT to engage with you, and the quickest route to generating those emotions is through imagery.

Think about these numbers for a second:

- 100 million users watch videos online every single day.
- 74% of social media marketers use visual assets in the social media marketing, ahead of blogs (68%) and videos (60%)

- 75% of smartphone owners watch videos on their phones EVERY DAY

(Source: Social Media Examiner Industry report)

Your dream customer is already unconsciously filtering all the content which is not relevant to them. To reach them, you need to be able to stop them in their tracks.

IF you're not making full use of all the amazing platforms available to you to WOW your customers with incredible images, you are not going to be doing yourself justice.

Let's take a look next at how we can STOP THE SCROLL and grab attention with your beautiful brand images...

CHAPTER 16

WHAT YOU NEED VISUAL IMAGERY FOR!

We all want to know how to STOP THE SCROLL behaviour on social media right? Even on websites and other online content, the SCROLL has become a habit that lots of business owners spend HOURS agonising over how to break.

As well as being business owners, we are all also consumers too, and probably all intuitively know the feeling. We KNOW how many feeds we will simply skip past as they are just not delivering what we need at that precise time. The images do not excite us. We don't feel that CONNECTION.

Luckily for us, there are some specific areas you can improve on, to make sure that your lovely brand IS one of the ones which commands attention!

It is all about creating, with intention, the RIGHT kind of images for your brand. Creating those stunning visuals which will transport your potential new customer out of their zombie-state of scrolling, scrolling and instantly put them in a place they want to be - asking questions, interested, wanting to find out more.

So here are my top tips for creating images that are going to be used on social media.

1 - RECOGNISABILITY

Your brand images HAVE to be instantly recognisable to anyone who comes across them. Your visual language needs to shout from the rooftops without saying a single word! We've talked already about consistency, and this is where it really comes into play. When you start to build a coherent visual style for all your brand images, it becomes your calling card.

You NEED your customers to recognise you ANYWHERE.

And when I say 'you', I do mean both you personally, and you as a brand. As we've already seen, you have as little as six seconds to make an impact on someone - you don't want to waste those precious seconds having your dreamy client wondering if they are looking at your brand or another one they were wondering about last week! Make your images uniquely YOURS.

Think for a minute about the feeds you love on Instagram. What is it about them that instantly lets you know through your scrolling that you're looking at your favourite brand of the moment? It could be something as simple as the subject matter - perhaps you follow them for their incredibly styled interiors shots. Or maybe they always use a really beautiful colour combination which resonates with you. I'd bet my life that the actual QUALITY of the images is always high - good resolution, sharp focus in the right areas etc.

When you're planning out your shoot, or how to use your images on social media, think about HOW your customers are going to recognise you - what is it about you, and your photos which will really set you apart from everybody else?

You need to foster that sense of familiarity with your loyal followers. DELIVER, time after time, the 100% emotional EXPERIENCE that they are seeking from your brand, and you will see how much power your images can create in your favour.

2 - STORY TELLING

Creating powerful images for social media is all about storytelling. Now that we know how important visual communications are in creating a narrative for your brand, you can start to craft exactly HOW you are going to achieve this with your social media images.

For every image you choose, or use, put yourself in the mind of your perfect customer and ask yourself:

> "**What is this image SHOWING me?**"

I don't mean literally - you can "show" a million different things physically in an image after all! I'm talking about the STORY the image is revealing to your audience. What does it tell them about right now? What point in their story is it picking up on? What questions does your image ask of the viewer?

If we want to make emotional connections through our images, you have to put yourself first in the place of the person you're trying to reach. IF you truly understand THEIR story, then it becomes the natural next step to start to expand it. To REVEAL how your brand will connect with them emotionally. To show, with a beautiful image, how you will meet their need.

The thing about stories is that they are always moving forwards. There's always a next step. It's this sense of ACTION and discovery that you can build with the right choice of images for your brand. You want your social media scroller to STOP. To TUNE IN, and take the action to click. To find out more.

To **DISCOVER**.

3 - IMPACT

You want to create a split second experience which will WOW your social media scroller, and draw them in. You want to show them EXACTLY the best life they could be living if they would only decide to buy your incredible product, or use your wonderful services. You want to show them vitality! Energy!

What's going to be the best type of image to do this? A mundane, run of the mill picture of your drinks bottle, snapped on your phone as you make your way to the gym? The gym involves energy, right?

WRONG!

Yes, going to the gym is an energetic thing, but there's nothing about your hasty, out of focus snap of a sports drink bottle which is going to create an EMOTIONAL response for your scroller. Why would they stop for this?! There's nothing more for them to experience here.

To create images for social media which have IMPACT, you first need to understand your scroller. KNOW your audience. It might be that all your intentions are in the right place, but the actual quality of your execution, your choice of shots is letting you down at the last minute.

Imagine the difference your scroller might have seen if instead of showing them your (static) drinks bottle, you'd presented them with a gorgeous shot of you, brimming with life and energy having just finished your gym session. You are beaming from ear to ear, and your enthusiasm is infectious.

You might look a little wild, maybe a bit flushed, or even a bit sweaty, but if your face was telling them the right story - that if you do what I do, you will look and feel GREAT - that's much more likely to have the desired effect of grabbing their attention.

Of course what images are going to have the most impact will be a matter for you to learn. Each brand is different after all. A lot will depend on your ideal customer too - what is going to get

THEM excited? Is it super high contrast, bold bright images? Or gentle, gorgeous romantic and atmospheric shots?

If the ideal client you need to reach is like you, a smart, focussed, busy woman for whom time is precious, your need to make sure that your images have immediate impact. That they DELIVER, time and time again, and don't waste a single opportunity to make those magical moments of connection.

In our next section we're going to take a much closer look at how and where you can use your images for MAXIMUM impact for your brand to truly STAND OUT.

PART 5

HOW TO USE YOUR IMAGES

CHAPTER 17

HOW TO USE IMAGES ON YOUR WEBSITE

My secret sauce

I am a big fan of websites that have a simplistic feel. Sites which are very direct and obvious about the journey you want your viewer to go through. Sites which are easy to use, easy to understand and easy to navigate through features.

Keeping it clean and crisp and SIMPLE is king, to help provide a clear view of the showcased item, service, product. Your images and the use of them on your website need to follow the same structure.

Here is a quick rundown of the bare minimum 3 images you have to use on your website.

1. Lots of negative space

> Create the feeling of space and light in your images, even if your website is about being dark and moody, create an atmospheric feel of what it is like to work with you by using a wide shot, negative space heavy image to grab attention.

2. Get Personal

Choose an incredible and emotional headshot for the win. A photograph that really shows your true features and characteristics, exactly what people will get when they meet you in person or skype with you online.

3. Go for the money shot

Create an image that screams you are the expert. That your offering will solve all their problems or AT LEAST THEIR MOST IMPORTANT ONE! Make this image approachable and professional and hot as! Make sure they know in no uncertain terms that you mean business, and that you are THE TOP DOG in what you do.

Landing Pages

If you are designing a landing page to specifically gather info e.g. an opt in for an email type transaction, then LESS IS MORE! Use a fabulous image of you or your offering and KEEP THE PAGE SIMPLE! No distractions!

Sales Pages

Are you launching a program or course? Or maybe you have a new package or service coming out and you need a sales page. Using images on this page is key.

Crowded, text heavy sales pages can be distracting and overwhelming, so be aware how your use of images can break up the blurb! I suggest having three images on this page, as well as a summary gallery of your product or service / experience. If you are including testimonials on this page, then please KEEP THEM ALL THE SAME SIZE AND SHAPE!! I so often see testimonials all over the place on sales pages, and this is confusing and messy!! It's super simple to drop testimonials into a template and upload that way, or use a pre-uploaded template directly on your website builder.

I use Squarespace to host my site, and it has great ability for consistency for content like this in the image block feature. Choose a shape - e.g. a square headshot or round headshot - whatever design element best fits your website and brand theme, and STICK TO IT! Keep everything tidy and organised so people can easily navigate and understand the information you are presenting them with.

Use your bare bones three images to really complement the experience you are providing from the sales page.

Commerce Pages

Product and service images are ALWAYS OVERLOOKED in importance. Ladies go to huge lengths and investments to bring their amazing products / service-based businesses to life and then at the FINAL HURDLE settle for mediocre or a lot of the time, darn right BAD photographs of their beloved offerings!

The key to GREAT and ENGAGING offering photographs is to KEEP IT SIMPLE.

Opt for plain white backgrounds that really showcase the product. Uniformity and consistency is key, and this is a clean and crisp way to show your product completely. If you are listing a product, for example something wearable, then show it worn!! Your buyers want to see what it is going to look like when they own it, and visualising how that look makes them feel is a huge help in the decision-making process.

Similarly if you are selling artwork, show your buyers how it is going to look in their home. Are you making a canvas for the wall? If so, show HOW can they expect that to look in their home. Give them the visual insight to the finished result and they will find the decision-making process so much easier!

Editorial Campaigns

Editorial type campaign images TELL A STORY via a sequence of images. These images are particularly important in order to VISUALLY convey the EXPERIENCE your offering provides to the client. You can really make this type of image series amazing by using unique and quirky personality traits of you and your brand to influence the concept and SHOWCASE your magnificence.

CHAPTER 18

HOW TO USE IMAGES ON YOUR SOCIAL MEDIA

So, this is going to be a really basic run down of MY favourite social media platforms and the best ways to use images to showcase your brand.

> **MINDSHIFT - YOU CAN NOT USE THE SAME IMAGE ON EVERY PLATFORM!**

> **MINDSHIFT - POORLY TAKEN SMARTPHONE SNAPS ARE NOT PROFILE PICTURE MATERIAL WHEN YOU ARE PLAYING WITH THE BIG BOYS!**

FACEBOOK

Now, Facebook is multifaceted - there are so many different places you can exist on Facebook that images, and lots of them, are imperative!

Your personal Facebook profile

Needs a STRONGLY RECOGNISABLE image for the profile picture. I understand that maybe you really desperately want to use that pic of you with your best friend, back when you'd had such a giggle falling out of a bar because it always makes you both smile, but think - is this really the best use of this wonderful opportunity to reach people with your brand?! Probably not.

Your Facebook personal profile pic should be instantly recognisable as YOU, but also, be a clear and consistent link to your brand. Even though you will have a separate, business area on Facebook for your biz, you really have to maximise every opportunity to live your brand, and your personal page is likely to be many people's first experience of you. Make it count!

I also recommend having a branded cover image on your personal Facebook page - whether that be a link to your Facebook community, or your recent opt-in, or maybe just your website. Utilising this space for the free marketing capacity it provides is a no brainer.

You can also make the most of the feature to use highlighted or featured images on your personal Facebook page too. Choose great shots which tell a story - whether it's about your overall brand, a special offer, an opt-in - anything which is going to intrigue and excite your personal connections and prompt them to click through to find out more.

Get into the habit of sharing directly from your business page onto your personal page too. The more exposure you can get across the various areas of Facebook, the more likeable and sharable your content is going to be. It's all about widening your reach, so you can talk to as many potential lovely new clients as possible!

Now I do understand that not everything you're going to be posting on your personal page is going to be able to be a professionally shot gorgeous image, but be mindful of what you are posting. Before you put anything on social media, think:

- o   What story is this telling my audience?
- o   What does this say about me? And therefore,
- o   What could this mean for my brand?

Once you truly start living your brand at every touchpoint, you're going to have much better sense of the RECOGNISABILITY of your images, and the STORY they tell.

Your Business "Like" Page

Again you need a STRONGLY RECOGNISABLE image for the profile picture. You can use the same picture as your personal profile page to keep consistency, and if you have only have a small amount of images at your disposal right now.

Your business page is where you really supercharge your branding. This is where people are expecting to find your best - the good stuff, which will really excite them! They KNOW they're looking at your brand, and it's up to you to make sure that the images and content you are showcasing here can really deliver. So use your best images. Make sure you are building the right narrative.

You can think of your business page as a support tool for your business. It's a great way to CONNECT with your audience, to engage with people who are ACTUALLY LOOKING TO BE ENGAGED! Let's face it, if you're spending time looking at a brand on Facebook, the chances are it's because you're intrigued - you WANT to get to know them better, to get a sense of WHO they are, and WHAT they can offer you right?

For sure your Cover Picture Space needs to be fully utilised, with either a link to your group, your opt-in or your web page. I suggest using a picture with plenty of negative space of either YOU or YOUR PRODUCT on the cover photo with a STRONG call to action!

There's lots of great ways you can use your biz page to talk directly to your audience, and these ways are increasing all the time. Use livestreams, stories, images, links, ads - Facebook has so many great ways to connect.

Another under-optimised use of your business page is sharing motivational quotes, hints and tips in a haphazard way. Its super easy to create a template in your brand colours which you can then write over the top any quotes etc. that you want to share PLUS you can include a small note of your website which when shared is great free marketing!

Facebook Stories

Following in the success of Instagram stories, Facebook stories can be a brilliant tool for reaching your audience quickly. They appear at the top of the feed, so if you're constantly keeping the content on there fresh, it's a great way to catch people's attention before they scroll off somewhere!

The great thing about Facebook stories is that you can use it to showcase your brand slightly differently. To show another angle on what you do. Because users have to click to view your story, I like to use stories to show more informal content and images - the kind of things you might not be sure would look right as a permanent fixture on your feed, but that still builds your credibility.

> **THINK: What else could your brand be saying here?**

For example, Facebook Stories are great for those 'behind the scenes' type images. Perhaps it's just a snapshot of your day, building the picture of who you are and what you're doing, working hard for your lovely clients. This is where you can lever your more personal content, the more laid back stuff. You still need to make sure that what you're posting on stories doesn't jar against the rest of your brand, but think of it as an opportunity to show your audience a sideways, rather than full on, view of your incredible brand.

This type of content can build intimacy and TRUST with your audience. It's so important for connection that your customers

BELIEVE in you. By inviting them along your brand journey in Facebook Stories, you can build this relatability more easily.

Facebook Groups

Now there's a number of reasons you might be joining groups on Facebook. They are exactly what they sound like - groups of people, who are all coming together for some shared purpose! Maybe you're already a member of some groups local to your area, you want to be part of the physical community of an area, and a Facebook Group is a great way to easily connect with those people. Or maybe you share a hobby or interest, and a group is a good way of sharing knowledge or expertise? Or maybe you use groups more strategically, to make connections in places or with people you're hoping to partner with.

The great thing about groups is they create a platform for CONVERSATION. Everyone is there to listen, as well as talk! Now it can be tempting to barge on in to a new group and start (metaphorically) shouting about yourself and how great your brand is, but the online world is not so different to the real world in this sense - you have to build the TRUST, and be respectful in a conversation, just like in real life!

The key to getting the most out of groups for your brand is to INTERACT. Join in! Talk to people, listen and comment on what they have to say. You will naturally connect with others in a group if you are personable. Just be YOU! You'll find that your group will get to know you - and by extension your BRAND - and you can tell your story in an authentic way.

The other great thing about groups is that everyone there already shares a purpose, so you can be much more strategic in tailoring your content for exactly what that audience needs. For your local area group for example, you're going to know that they are much more likely to be interested in hearing about your new exhibition or local event than the people in your 'hobby/interest' group, who actually would respond better to some content sharing your expertise, and positioning yourself as a go-to resource.

Tell your STORY

On all the various areas of Facebook - your personal profile, your business page, your groups and your stories - you have to create a compelling BRAND STORY. You have this great versatile platform to bring your visuals to life in a meaningful way. So the images and the content that you're sharing with your (growing!) audience needs to speak to them WHERE THEY ARE. You can REVEAL different aspects of your brand, depending on which area of the platform you're communicating on, but throughout all of it, the golden rule is to be CONSISTENT.

Your images are going to speak so strongly to your audience, so it's really worth spending the time to craft a rock solid brand foundation here.

INSTAGRAM: THE CURATION PLATFORM

Instagram is all about what you have on the outside. It is definitely a judge a book by the cover platform.

Your images NEED to be strong enough in suggestion of STORY to stand alone without a caption until clicked. They need to DRAW in your target client from a simple enticing insight into the world of you.

So, HOW do you achieve this?

Well this really is very simple...

        Create Images your AUDIENCE WANT TO SEE!

Give them what they want.

Know what they desire from your business and show it to them.

Instagram gives you an amazing outlet where getting nitty, gritty and behind the scenes is what it is all about. It allows you to get raw with your audience and show them really what drives your day to day business. But the key point not to forget is:

You need to SHOW THEM WHAT THEY WANT TO SEE

So, for example, if you are targeting really techy social media loving audience - they probably don't want to know what you had for breakfast - this isn't going to get them to stop their scroll. However in your Instagram stories, you can quite naturally show what you had for breakfast and how you start off your work day.

If you are a health guru then your followers are going to LOVE your gorgeous organic breakfast photographs, and this IS going to stop their scroll. Whereas if you put up a load of techy, marketing statistics in a graphic - that's probably going to turn them right off.

Stick to what you KNOW your target market LOVE and then show them every single in and out of it!

Your Instagram feed allows you to show the reality of your business - ALL of the INS, and ALL of the OUTS, so you can really showcase and highlight the unique experience that your clients get and LOVE from you and your business.

Instagram Stories allow you to go even deeper and show the reality of how YOU go about making that day in the life of your business happen.

My top tips for a FABULOUS Instagram Account

- Use a clear and close up profile image so your tribe can find and recognise you instantly.

- Curate your content - LOOKS DO MATTER ON INSTAGRAM! Plan out your content in a visually appealing way so that your feed is gorgeously delicious and tempting to all those new followers checking you out.
- Pick a theme and stick to it!! Whether it's a filter you use ALL THE TIME, or a frame shape, size or colour you just love, make a choice and keep it consistent.
- Make sure EVERY image you use is brand specific and recognisable. Don't be tempted by quick fix colours or items that don't make strategic brand sense to you and your business. Create your own stock image bank so you always have GORGEOUS and UNIQUE images to use when you have something to say.
- Utilize the highlights roll feature - Simply repurpose a recent Insta Stories image to the highlights roll to draw more attention to what you got going on.

FILTER AND FUNNEL

So now we've learned a little more about two of the main social platforms and how best to boost your profiles on there, just stop for a minute. We need to sense check WHY we're doing all this!

What is your social media FOR?!

Your social media, your profiles, your activity, your content should all be part of your strategy to FILTER AND FUNNEL your potential clients into exactly where you need them to be. You can use your images to take people from one place to another.

Optimising your profiles is so important to draw people in to what your brand can offer them. We want to be ENGAGING them, exciting them first, and then - and here's the important part - GIVING THEM A CLEAR DIRECTION TO GO NEXT!

It's all well and good having a beautiful business page, but if there is no ACTION for your interested audience to take next, then you are missing out on an opportunity!

By mapping out who the various platforms are engaging you with, you can understand WHERE you want to take them, to get them to convert that love and excitement you've made them feel with your gorgeous brand images, and turn it into sales!

It's all part of the process:

Use your images to challenge and excite, then…

Filter your audience, take them to…

The right LINK, for them to…

ENGAGE, and take ACTION!

Facebook and Instagram are GREAT ways to establish these connections. All the platforms also have ads which you can use to target people even further. The level of detail you can get from a Facebook ad is unbelievable, so you can know exactly who you're talking to, and filter your messaging and your creative just for them.

When you are filtering and funnelling all your lovely prospects, keep in mind the three important checkpoints we learned about earlier when you're planning out your images and brand content. You need to be:

1. Instantly recognisable. BE your brand, STAND OUT, let people know EXACTLY who they are talking to!

2. Telling the right story. What is it that this person needs and desires, and HOW are you giving it to them?

3. Be impactful. Create stunning, high quality and CONSISTENT images which will blow their socks off!

By hitting these three focus areas, and keeping them front of mind when you're using social platforms like Facebook and Instagram, you're very quickly going to build that CREDIBILITY for your brand that money can't buy!

Once you establish with your audience that they can trust you to always deliver exactly what they need, you can start to position yourself as the authority, and up level your brand to bigger and more incredible things! We'll look at this in a little more detail later on.

Now that we have your online world all figured out, in the next section, we're going to think about how you can create STAND OUT impact with your printed materials too.

CHAPTER 19

HOW TO USE IMAGES ON PRINTED MATERIALS

> **MINDSHIFT - A BUSINESS CARD NEEDS TO NOT BE YOUR ONLY PRINTED MATERIAL!!**

We've spent a lot of time already thinking about all the amazing ways you can connect and grow your audience online. Now you're going to need to consider what you're actually doing in the real, physical world too, to make your brand STAND OUT!

It can be tempting to think that print is all a bit old fashioned. And it's true, lots of people DO manage to build great businesses by just focussing on online activity. But there is SO much you can do to really create an impact with the physical brand assets you create, that to dismiss it completely is missing a trick, in my opinion.

Let's take a look at some of the staples your brand might need, and how you can use your images to get the most out of printed materials for your business.

My overall tip?

KEEP IT SIMPLE!!!

Business Cards

Yes they are a staple for any business person who meets with people who may become in some way a lead or partner to the business they have created.

Yes they have a lot of necessary, every day, and ordinary information on - this does not mean they have to be any of those things!!

For me, personal preference when it comes to business cards is to:

- Choose a thick card stock, and then have a lamination to achieve a more touchy feely effect. You can get this in velvet or in gloss so it really works for the majority of brands. If you're more eco-minded and earthy, then a natural thick card stock with its gorgeous natural rugged texture will give the same effect.
- Keep. It. Simple!! I love a dash of colour and literally the bare minimum text.
- I include my name and my website, then my logo and my title on the flip side.

That's it. All of my contact details are on my website so check it out and call me. So business cards can do a very simple job. But what else could you create which is really going to make your brand stand out?

Compliments slips

The things which are really going to make your brand STAND OUT in the minds of your customers are the little things. The things which yes, it would be easy not to do, maybe nobody bothers any more. But imagine the difference in EMOTIONS you can create for your lovely customers if they really feel you are taking the time to care about every single detail.

If you were sent a package, imagine how special a handwritten compliments slip would feel to receive. You'd feel that someone had taken the time to notice you, the individual customer. You'd feel CARED for. You would feel NOTICED.

It doesn't need to be anything wildly complicated - remember, the golden rule is to keep things simple, but creating a simple comp slip with either one of your gorgeous images on, or perhaps just your simple brand/logo can make the difference between what you are sending being noticed for the right reasons.

Banners

Perhaps you're thinking of attending a trade show for your industry. Being present in person like this can be a great way to connect first hand with people, but you need to make sure that every aspect of how you present yourself at a show is in line with your brand and identity.

Think - what sort of message would it send out if you were looking at a trade stand where they had no visual brand identity. Everything was cobbled together on home printed signs with no colour, visuals or any kind of co-ordination. You'd probably feel like maybe this person didn't really VALUE their offering very highly right?

Now, imagine the difference in first impressions where you come across a stand who has a gorgeous banner, which clearly shows their brand name, and immediately draws you in with an image which speaks to you, and lets you know what you can expect in terms of quality, and value if you were to go over and find out more. You'd be much more likely to engage with that brand.

> **MINDSHIFT- THINK ABOUT WHAT CAN BE SEEN!**

If you're going to be representing your brand at a busy event in a packed hall, there's no point having your main message right down at the bottom of a vertical pull up banner, because no-one is going to be able to read it! Especially if people are crowding around your stall, think about what content will still be visible, even if someone is standing in front of it.

You want to keep any important messaging above head height if it is what's going to speak to someone across a crowded room. In the same way, keep in mind the size of text you're using. (This goes for all printed materials).

Is it easy to read? If not, people probably won't bother to read it! It's all well and good falling in love with a beautifully flowing detailed script font, and this might work really well for a headline, or key message but be far too difficult to read if it's appearing across 5 paragraphs of content in size 8pt!

Make it personal

For me, I've always gone for very simple, lovely big images of the person behind the business on my banners. You want people to immediately feel that sense of connection to you and your brand. It's also really important to tailor the images you choose to what you are trying to achieve. Keep in mind WHO you will be talking to at that particular point in your journey too - is it totally new customers, who have no idea about who you are or what you have to offer? Or is it people who you've already engaged with, who might need to dive a little deeper into what your brand has to offer them.

Bespoke print

Just because you haven't done it before, doesn't mean it shouldn't be done! One of the best parts of running your own incredible legacy business is the freedom to create EXACTLY whatever your heart can dream up!

If you're doing stuff offline, make the most of the creative opportunities that presents! Are you trying to target a particular kind of high end customer? Why not create something completely bespoke and personalised just for them?! So many people are running businesses online these days, that actually, to physically create and send something WOULD set you and your brand apart.

It could be anything, from a mini magazine with beautifully shot and styled images, through to a gorgeously crafted little taster of what you have to offer, along with a glossy invitation and hand tied ribbon. Let your imagination run wild - if you can think it, you can do it! The trick is as always to put yourself in the shoes of your dream customer. What would THEY be delighted to receive? What would make THEM sit up and take notice?

Touch is important

If you're creating something in print that's going to be repping your brand in the real world, not just online, you need to consider not just what content goes on it, but also how it will physically FEEL. There's such a huge choice of stock and finishes when it comes to printing materials. It can be hard to know where to start, but don't be limited to just what you've seen in the past.

Talk to your printer about what finishes could help set you apart. Maybe a touch of spot gloss laminate would give your brochure a polished, professional feel? Or perhaps for a special thick card stock personalised invitation, you might opt for a gold emboss, to add that VIP touch.

You can tailor the stock you choose to the kind of audience you're trying to reach with each communication. If your brand is about natural, eco-friendly earthy vibes, then an uncoated, unbleached card is going to be a better choice than a glossy, high colour laminated finish.

Think about what your audience will appreciate.

AUTHORITY AND CONNECTION

The common thread running through all of this is about using what you have, what your brand STANDS FOR, to build a rock solid connection to your dream audience.

When you meet their deepest desires, when you wow them and draw them in to your brand with your gorgeous images, your whole brand will make the right impact in the mind of your dream client.

How do we do this?

Simple. We BUILD it, one step at a time. You don't have to do it all at once. As we've seen, especially online, you have to EARN the trust of your customers, by SHOWING UP, time and time again. You build the trust that your brand is going to meet their needs. That you have what they want. That your brand IS what they desire.

This trust is only going to come if you are consistent in your identity. You're going to create these incredible connections with your audience, and they in turn, will keep on coming back to your brand.

So you keep it fresh. You keep delivering them this great content that they've come to love and expect from you. Your images tell the beautiful story of what your brand MEANS, and it never gets old, because there's always something new to discover.

Eventually, what happens is that you can start to up-level your brand, to a position of AUTHORITY. You BECOME the expert in your particular area. Your customers know this - because they've seen it from you over and over again! - and they trust you to deliver.

Your CONNECTION builds your AUTHORITY

From this position of authority, you can start to open up new opportunities, and really take your brand to the next level. You can scale up your offering. You can speak with new confidence to the next level of client you want to talk to. You are constantly ADAPTING through the whole process so that your brand is always EXACTLY where you need it to be.

When you position yourself and your brand as the go-to, as the experts in what you are doing, you will truly see transformations in your business that you once might never have dreamed could be possible.

SUMMARY

So how about it, legacy building lady?! Are you ready to truly STAND OUT? Both online, on social and in the real world you're gaining all the tools you need to take your brand to the stratosphere and beyond!

In the next section, we're going to get right into the details of how to plan the most incredible shoot. Let's get to it!

PART 6

PLANNING YOUR PERSONAL BRANDING PHOTOSHOOT

CHAPTER 20

PREPARING FOR A BRAND SHOOT

This next section is designed to help you understand the steps you need to take to prepare for a branding photoshoot for your business.

The main consideration you need to be crystal clear on is WHAT you are going to be using the photographs for. It is a really common theme amongst businesses owners they have a few headshots taken for use on social media, and then neglect the other vital ways they can utilise photography throughout their business.

> **MINDSHIFT: YOU NEED MULTIPLE SHOOTS DEPENDING ON WHAT YOU ARE SELLING!**

Question no. 1 - What is it for? What are you selling? Who are you selling it to?

Getting to grips with the purpose of the shoot is the first hurdle. Understanding you can shoot for a specific website sales page - maybe you have printed marketing material and you have a high ticket event planned - you will need to shoot specifically to sell this event.

I agree with repurposing images IF they convey the correct story and IF they have relevance to the product or service which you are currently selling.

For example, maybe you have launched an online course recently and you now have plans for an in-person masterclass event. This is going to need a different *feel* of image, to give your viewers the FEELING that they are going to experience from working with you 1-2-1. This type of event is likely to have a higher price tag and your customers are investing more deeply in you. You need to reassure and reaffirm the feeling your experience will give them, as well as your promise and devotion to seeing that through.

You also need to highlight the spectacular location you may have chosen for your in-person event. Maybe you are flying off to sunnier climates and need gorgeous location images, as well as a welcoming and personalised feeling with you included.

Think about each shoot as a campaign - yes you can repurpose the images on social media BUT my top tip is to plan out your product / service offerings for the upcoming 12 months and work out how many photography shoots you need to invest in in order to support those campaigns.

Question 2 - What does the mood / feel need to be?

The next point to consider now you know WHAT you are selling and the purpose of the shoot, is what MOOD and feel is it going to need?

Are you selling something sensitive like a breakthrough retreat that will need to be gorgeously optimistic, bright and open as well as safe and secure?

Taking the time to really understand the offering you are designing the campaign shoot for will help you communicate with your dreamy target audience.

Understanding mood also means thinking whether your shoot needs to feel intimate and vulnerable, or whether you need to be presented as an authoritative expert. Maybe you need a mixture of both for this specific campaign?

Question 3 - What location will work best?

The next sensible step from deciding the mood of your photo shoot is to look at location. Is this all about telling the story of you and your business and how you came to be? Are you revamping your website about page and social media presence? Maybe you are selling a breakthrough retreat, so the location of the retreat is a huge part of the story of the campaign.

Locations don't always have to be a huge expense. You can find lovely little gems right on your doorstep. Look for beautiful architecture, sleek modern and contemporary design or just a lovely little garden cafe. Hotel lounges also are a great choice, easily accessible and thanks to the world of travel bloggers, are usually very accommodating to shooting in their establishments.

The important thing to get right is that your location tells the right story for the purpose of the shoot. If it's a major shoot you want for some hero images for your website, it is worth considering making the location equally as important. I've had clients choose destinations all over the world, as they knew that in order to perfectly capture what they were all about, they needed a beautiful destination to capture people's imagination. However, it's just as good to choose an interesting location close to home, if what you need are relatable images.

Who are the pictures going to speak to? And what will your audience relate to seeing? Time spent scoping out your potential locations is never wasted. You'll get a much better sense of what shots you could achieve, or perhaps see interesting quirks which could be a brilliant backdrop, or details which would work well for close ups.

I have a few top tips to consider when planning the location for your shoot.

1. Light, light, LIGHT!!

It's so obvious - great lighting is the cornerstone of great images! We all know how ageing bad lighting can be - think of the worst overhead fluorescently-lit changing room you've ever been in. I'll bet it didn't make you feel any joy at all looking in the mirror, and you probably were even less likely to BUY what you were trying on.

The best possible light for a shoot is light which meets the face from the side on. Overhead lighting can cast the face into shadow, changing proportions and adding years to your face. If your location is outside, try to find somewhere with overhead cover, like tree canopies, or an awning or arbour. This will diffuse the overhead sunlight a little.

Lots of clients have a particular café or cute venue they love, which at a first glance would seem to be the perfect venue - interesting décor, buzzing atmosphere etc. - but these types of venues can be really dingy! Yes that industrial style bare light bulb might look great while you're in there, but when it comes to create the perfect conditions for a shoot, these 'cosy' venues can be challenging.

2. Shooting indoors

If you decide to do a shoot indoors, there are a few other things to bear in mind as well as lighting. Firstly, think about the size of your chosen venue - if it's a busy café, because you want to show a particular kind of lifestyle shot for example, you'll need to consider the other customers. Will you need permission from your venue? Will they allow you to reserve a part of the place for your sole use? What about other users in the venue seeing your shoot in action?

3. Access and safety

Simply put, you have to be sure that you and your team will be safe and relaxed during your shoot. Now, all locations have different things to be aware of, but at a minimum you should think about the potential hazards you might encounter. If you're outside in public, make sure you're not blocking roads or access. What is the neighbourhood like? If it's crowded and busy, how will you make sure none of your stuff 'wanders off' while you're busy shooting? I know it's not a nice thing to think about, but especially in big cities where as we know stories of pickpocketing and theft are common, make sure you have a plan for keeping yourself and your equipment safe at all times.

4. Be location efficient!

Finally, when you're choosing a location for your shoot, think about how versatile it is. It's no good planning an atmospheric shoot on the steps of a romantic ruin, if you also need some indoor shots and there's no other civilisation for miles around! Time is precious on a shoot, and to get the most out of your day, or days, try to find locations with a variety of backdrops all within a close range of each other.

So, now we know WHERE we are shooting, we can move on to planning the next important thing: what to wear!

Question 4 - How to plan a shoot wardrobe?

Next, you need to think about wardrobe. Wardrobe styling is always a HUGE concern for the women I work with. Whether it's your first ever shoot, or you're a seasoned pro who does four shoots a month, what you are wearing is one of the biggest factors which contributes to the overall success of the shoot.

Think about it - that feeling you get on the inside when you've got your favourite outfit on, when you're feeling great, confident, and like you can take on the world? That shines through in your face, right?!

But there's more to choosing a wardrobe for a shoot than simply clothes that make you feel good. By following a few key rules, you can make sure you don't fall into common mistakes which could mean you don't maximise the success of your images. If you're working with a creative photographer who really understands what you need, the chances are like me they will have a style guide ready and prepared for you, to help you pick out the right type of outfit, depending on what you're looking to achieve.

Here are my top tips for wardrobe success:

1. Keep it simple!

Now simple doesn't have to mean 'boring'! For most people, unless you are a fashion blogger who is constantly making changes to keep up with trends and seasons, the best way to create an impact is with simple, classic, timeless outfits.

Think about where your images will be ending up, and realistically how long you'll expect them to be there. You don't want to be choosing seasonal, trend led pieces like the latest trouser shape or tricky neckline if you don't want your images to look dated after a few months.

Likewise, fabrics prints and colours can very easily date from one season to another. Stick with classic prints which never go out of style, or simple blocks of colour.

2. Dress for your shape

Now I KNOW everyone has hang-ups about their body. You've probably spent a lifetime buying clothes to cover up - or not cover up, if you're lucky! - those areas you don't feel comfortable with. You know what you feel comfortable in. The shapes you gravitate towards.

For example, if you're a curvy lady, you might always choose looser shapes which hide your shape. But a common mistake I see clients making is thinking that their failsafe 'comfortable' outfit is actually making the most of their assets!

A good photographer will be able to guide you towards clothing which will make the most of your natural shape, not hide it! It's about sculpting your body, to create the best SHAPE possible. This might mean trying clothes or styles that you've not worn before, but this is why it's so important to TRUST your photographer - after all, their job is to make you look great, and they do this for a living so know what works! Believe them!!

By playing with light and shade, colour pops and darker shades, a good stylist will be able to manipulate the viewers eye to where we want their attention to be. For example, for curvier clients, sculpting the hip area with a simple, dark pencil skirt draws the eye upwards. You can play with proportions with peplum tops, which skim the hips and create a great shape, or add interest higher up the body with well-chosen accessories.

The key is to KNOW your shape. Once you know it, you can work WITH it, not against it!

3. Accessorize!

Jewellery can work to bring in pops of colour, add personality, but also to break up areas of the body. For example, for larger chested ladies, a big chunky statement necklace is great for creating good proportions and adding interest.

Think too about the kind of impression you want your accessories to make. If you're going for a shoot for to promote a major event with a high price tag, you probably want to create a slick, professional impression. So even if naturally you really love giant, oversized pompom earrings, they're probably not going to be the best choice to create that impression. Save them for projects and shoots where you want to appear more relaxed and carefree. Better to choose classic, clean lines, which will promote a feeling of quiet, calm confidence in this case.

4. Colour

Similarly, the colours you choose to wear can have a huge impact on the feel of your shoot. You need to consider the location you're shooting in, and how the colours are going to work with the backdrop.

Are you shooting against a white brick wall? Your cream top is going to make you look like part of it, instead of standing out!

Also, consider how the colours or fabrics you wear for your shoot are going to work with your brand. What do the fabrics say about WHO you are? Is your brand relaxed, breezy, easy going? Then loose cotton, linens and textures can work well. But if what you need is crisp, clean lines for a pulled-together and polished brand, you need to have an idea of which finishes and textures might be better suited - silks, perhaps, or a simple leather pencil skirt.

You can also create certain moods with the colours you wear, and play with colour combinations. For example, red with black creates a very striking, quite formal and sharp look, whereas pairing the red with primary brights like yellow, or blue creates a much more relaxed and playful look.

5. Trust your photographer

I've touched on this already, but it's so important to communicate with your creative well before the shoot takes place. Discuss your ideas. Bring along your mood boards, pin looks that you like or clothing and styles you're drawn to. Is there a particular celebrity who has nailed the style of image you want to capture? I have curated an entire studio of dresses of every shape, size, colour and fit over the years for my clients, and the chances are any good photographer will be able to bring wardrobe ideas to the table to bring out the best in you. After all, that's why you're here right?!

6. Finally, don't burn out!

Actually doing a shoot can be an exhausting business! There's the travel, hair and makeup, outfit change after outfit change, touch-ups, holding poses...even for professionals, it can be hard work!

If you are crystal clear before you plan your shoot on what your content schedule is, and how you are going to use the images, you'll be able to make sure you get the shots you need. I always advise clients to start with two or three outfits for your first shoot, and then build from there. The more experience you have, the more you'll be able to find styles that work for you, and build a great library of totally WOW images for your lovely brand.

So, now you're looking good, let's think about...

Question 5 - What style of image are you shooting?

In the planning stages for a shoot, you HAVE to keep coming back to the question

"What is this shoot FOR?"

We've already touched on what the mood and feel should be. Now you need to think about what style of images you are going to need. Do you need something really formal, to present a pin-sharp, glossy image? Or maybe it's a documentary shoot, behind the scenes for a new product you're launching? Or perhaps you're aiming for a lifestyle shoot your dreamy customer is going to LOVE.

The more thinking you can do before the shoot of what the ENERGY needs to be, the better. It helps to bring as much to the planning as you can, so if that's Pinterest mood boards, or just prompt words with emotions you need to convey - HAPPY! STYLISH! LUXURIOUS! - then that will set the tone for the images you create.

You also need to know how many images you are aiming for. Maybe the primary goal is to get images for your web launch, but you're hoping to be able to repurpose some of the content for your social media. How many social posts will you need? And how often will you be posting them out? Is there a product or item you must have in shot?

If you take the time to think about all this in the planning stages, you are well on the way to a successful shoot.

Question 6 - Which props should I use?

Now obviously props can take a shoot from feeling one way to something completely different. Think about those photo booths you get at parties and gatherings - they usually come with a range of crazy and fun props like wigs, hats, inflatable pineapples, giant glasses.... If you saw an image with any of these props in, you'd immediately get the feeling which comes with them; a feeling of wild abandon, of fun, of being social and having a giggle with friends.

Props can be a powerful tool to cement the feelings you want your lovely audience to feel. I'm not suggesting an inflatable pineapple is always going to be right for you, but I guarantee that for any style of shoot, a good photographer will be able to guide to as to which props may help.

Perhaps you'll need a laptop, to show you at work on the go?

Or maybe a bunch of beautiful freshly cut flowers, to give a sense of lightness, of spring and possibilities.

Whatever props you choose, try to make sure they are in line with your overall brand. For example, if your shoot is outdoors and it's likely to be raining, take the time to source an umbrella in your brand colour palette. It's really nice to include personal props too, to show a little more of WHO you are and WHAT your wonderful brand is all about. What could you bring along to the shoot which will create the perfect story for your brand?

Your props should showcase your unique brand personality, so take the time to make sure they are absolutely perfect for you. Is your brand slick, and high tech? Make sure you're not shooting you making calls holding a ten-year-old phone with a broken screen! If it's shots of your beautiful creative studio, make sure the items you include in the background tell the right story - no messy paperwork, only beautiful, stylish products.

A good photographer will be able to help guide you on what props to use, and how to be natural about it. For my clients, I keep a prop library of basic items, and as part of shoot preparation make sure that the props we are using are suitable and will work with the chosen location.

Question 7 - Who else will be involved?

So you've found your location, planned your wardrobe, prepped every aspect of what you and your lovely creative need to achieve. The one thing a lot of people forget to consider is - what about other people?!

It's rare that people become wildly successful without support, input and teamwork with a wide range of people. Consider:

"Is there anyone else I should be including in my shoot?"

On a basic level, this could be something as simple as who is in the background of your images. If you want to show vibrancy, and energy, you can often achieve this by shooting in a busy venue, but you will need to think about exactly WHO will be in the background, and what sort of message THEIR image, dress, "props" and expressions will convey. Are they studious? Chatting? Serious and concentrating? Or laughing with friends?

It can also be nice to give your audience a bit of context in a shoot, to show the people who make up your team. This is a great way to build your brand story, and share the love a bit. This doesn't just have to be people - perhaps your business revolves around caring for animals, in which case it totally makes sense that you'd include your OWN pets in your shoot. What better way of really SHOWING your audience that you understand how precious THEIR pets are, by showcasing the love and affection you have for your own.

Question 8 - Building a library

No we're not talking here about the bricks and mortar kind. Big brand success means having a curated collection of stock images which perfectly represent your wonderful brand. When planning your brand shoot, a lot of the focus will be spent planning how you, as the business owner, will be presented.

However, it's also extremely important to build in the opportunity on your shoot to capture those types of multi-purpose image which can be used in a wide range of contexts.

> **MINDSHIFT - THE WHOLE OF YOU DOES NOT NEED TO BE IN EVERY SHOT!**

You can still achieve beautiful images, which DO include you, but only involve a close up of a part of your body. For instance, your perfectly manicured hands, writing down notes in your beautiful leather bound notebook. Or a macro close up shot of the gorgeous flowers you keep on your desk.

The devil is in the detail, so think before you shoot about what else your location, or your product could offer. You have to create images which are MORE than the sum of their parts - your detail stock images need to be part of the ongoing brand story - where are you going next? What happens to these products? Who else uses them? Which other items will bring the feelings to life you want to evoke in your dreamy customer?

It also goes without saying here that **CONSISTENCY IS KEY!**

Your stock images should be of the same tone, weight and style if you really want your brand to be instantly recognisable. Perhaps you are an all-natural brand, and go for a bleached out, scandi-feel. Or maybe your gorgeous brand is all about passion, energy and vibrancy - your stock images might all be bold, bright jewel tones, rich in colour so they really POP.

Whatever style of image you choose, making sure you are keeping true to your brand and staying consistent is so, so important.

SUMMARY

So, there's a lot to take in when it comes to preparing for the perfect shoot! From clothes, to colours, to props to people - not just taking the time, but MAKING the time to be clear on what you need to achieve is a sure-fire way to getting the brilliant brand images your business deserves, and showing you off in the BEST possible light to all your gorgeous customers.

In the next section, we're going to look at the creative people who actually make this happen, and how to communicate effectively all the brilliant plans you have made. Ready?!

CHAPTER 21

HOW TO COMMUNICATE WITH YOUR CREATIVES

Employing ANYONE ANYWHERE in your business is a big thing. It is a commitment, it is exciting and concerning all at the same time. Know that no one woman, has ever single-handedly built a legacy business empire. Attracting and employing those who bring out the best in you, and help you bring out the best in your business, is an all-round win-win situation.

It's important to work with another individual who always wants to excite and reward both you and your business, and the better at communicating and understanding you and the communication process they are, the easier the whole thing will be. Communicating efficiently and effectively, agreeing to everything clearly, transparently and in advance lets your creative do their very best to bring your dreams to life.

Common struggles in communication I see include:

- Not clearly communicating goals - how the end product is to look, feel and sound
- Too much advice
- Failure to give any advice
- Being surprised by the outcome

Being disappointed by the outcome

Appreciate the skills of your creative - after all, they are an expert in their field, so give them respect and room to breathe! Understand that there is a process. The good news is that by keeping the following things in mind, you will be able to make sure you're on the same page as your creative, and the results will be exactly what you need.

MINDSHIFT - SPEAK EMOTIONALLY

As we now know, we're aiming to produce an emotive response in our dreamy customer. We want them to feel an immediate connection with your brand. So to brief your creative, you need to also use this emotional language, to make them aware that you're trying to build a FEELING with your audience.

You can be quite literal in describing how you want your audience to respond. Think about what language will help your creative understand the connection. How can you convey the desired client response? By using emotional language in your briefings, you will get emotional connection in the output.

MINDSHIFT - WEB/ GRAPHIC / PHOTO / VIDEO DESIGNERS ARE ARTISTS AS WELL AS BUSINESS PEOPLE

In any creative process you need to keep an open mind. Yes, when it comes to briefing a creative, YOU are the client, but don't forget the reason you're briefing them in the first place - FOR THEIR CREATIVITY! You might have a very clear idea in your mind of how your finished images will look, but trust that your creative will also bring valuable ideas to the table.

Give them the freedom to inspire you! Be open to suggestions. People who are creative for a living often will bring perspectives that you might never have thought of. By keeping an open mind, and being prepared to flex your initial ideas, together you can create something very special, which will be completely unique to you and your brand.

MINDSHIFT - CREATIVES ARE NOT MIND READERS

A thorough briefing for you creative is so, SO important! If ever in the past you have been disappointed with the result of a creative process, think back to what you briefed. Did you explain clearly your audience, aims, objectives and vision for success? Were you clear on what you expected to be delivered as a final result? Did you present your vision to the creative in a variety of ways - by explaining, in writing, with mood boards, with images? Did you check back they understood your brand?

EVERYONE brings their own personal interpretation to even the most basic of instructions. For example: Think of a blue triangle next to a red circle. Simple, right? But you gave this brief to three different designers, you might get three completely different versions back! Perhaps the shade of the blue would differ. The triangle might be bigger than the circle, or smaller. One designer might have the triangle on the left, one might have it on the right. One might have added drop shadows, or added perspective. One might have added a border around the image. One might have set up the file for print, one for web.

When talking to creatives, remember that what they picture in their minds eye when you explain something might look different to how you see it in yours. If you are aware of this, and can be open and flexible to possibility, you're much more likely to be delighted with what your designer creates for you.

MINDSHIFT - YOUR DESIGNER NEEDS TO CREATE FOR YOUR DREAMY CLIENT

At the end of the process, who will be paying your creative? You! So who do you think your creative is going to have in mind when they are working on your project? Yep, you guessed it - you. Your ACTUAL AUDIENCE might not be front of mind at all times, because ultimately, they will be designing for your approval.

But, you need to make sure you thoroughly road test any creative with the actual AUDIENCE it is intended for. Now obviously, you have to love it too! But the feedback you get from the people around you, your partner, your friends etc., whilst it is all valuable, must take second place to the feedback from the RIGHT people.

Make sure your creative understands who these people are, and brief them to keep the end clients' needs, wants and desires prioritised while they are working on your brand.

> **MINDSHIFT - CLEAR AND OPEN RELATIONSHIPS AROUND MONEY, HOURS AND TIME ARE VITAL**

I know that for a lot of people, talking about the nitty gritty of money can feel difficult sometimes. I'm here to tell you that you, awesome legacy building lady, are NOT going to be one of them! Never be afraid to talk frankly and clearly about money, costs and boundaries with your creative.

It comes down to respecting the people you're doing business with, valuing their time, and appreciating the skill set they have as one you need, and being prepared to pay for it. Believe me when I say that most creatives will appreciate an up-front discussion about costs, rather than payment being treated as an embarrassing afterthought!

As creative people, what they are selling is their time - not just the time spent on your job, but actually the unseen years and years of study, practice, experimentation, failures and successes which ENABLE them to show up and ace your project first time!

There's a great analogy where a factory owner calls out an engineer to fix a machine which has broken. The engineer shows up, looks at the machine for a minute, takes out a spanner and tightens a nut. The machine sputters to life! He writes out his bill, then turns to leave, having been in the building for less than five minutes. The bill is for a thousand pounds! The factory owner begins to query how the engineer can possibly justify such a cost for such a short time, so the engineer writes another bill. This one is broken down into just two lines and says "Cost for tightening the nut: £1. Cost for knowing WHICH nut to tighten: £999"

Creative work is no different. It takes years of experience to be able to know, in an instant what a client needs! Be the perfect client who values that experience.

MINDSHIFT - IT'S NOT ALL FOR YOUR DESIGNER TO DO

We've already talked about the importance of a great brief. But there will be other things that your lovely designer will need from you, in order to create the results that you want. Be prepared to do your research, to be able to give your creative a great background in what your brand is all about.

Some creatives might have additional briefing documents they'll ask you to fill out. They might ask you to research alternative options to your initial brief. Or create additional mood boards before your shoot.

It's also very important to take the time to give clear and detailed feedback, in the event that there are amends or changes you'd like the creative to make. Saying "I just don't like it" might be true, but is not really going to help the designer know where to start making changes! Try and frame your feedback in a constructive way, with tangible action points to help guide your creative towards what you really want to be seeing.

MINDSHIFT - ORGANISATION FOR THE WIN

For some people, being organised seems to come naturally. For others, it's a constant battle to remember where to find the form you need, which deadlines need action next, or even what those deadlines were for!

It comes down to this - whether you find it easy, or find it hard, the only way you're going to get organised is if you MAKE the time to get organised! It's not going to happen by accident! We so often make excuses for ourselves, saying we simply don't have the time to keep things in order. But when you think about organisation in terms of PRIORITES, lots of these excuses fall apart.

We all have the same number of hours in the day, after all! Think about some of the non-urgent tasks you might be prioritising without even realising it. Absent-mindedly scrolling through social media, even if you have a deadline to meet? Slumping on the sofa watching TV after a long day instead of listening to that podcast you've been meaning to get round to for ages? Colour-coding your stationery draw instead of actually writing that creative brief?!

We've all done it, but when you recognise that you CAN prioritise being organised - keeping to a schedule, setting up a great system so you can easily locate all your important stuff, replying to important messages straight away instead of putting it off - you'll see a huge increase in your results, as well as your peace of mind.

MINDSHIFT - SEEK FEEDBACK FROM YOUR IDEAL CLIENT! NO ONE ELSE IS QUALIFIED TO GIVE AN OPINION!

We touched on this earlier, but the opinions on your creative which really matter are the ones of your audience. It's often too tempting, especially when you're just starting out, or nervous about 'putting yourself out there' to only seek out those 'soft' audiences which you know will probably give you positive feedback. It can be a great ego boost when your entire family LOVE your new logo after all.

But as we know, we're not here building brands just to feed our ego! We need to keep a focus on building a brand which is RIGHT for our dreamy client. So try to seek out those opinions which will REALLY make a difference to your growth. Even when they might not be the message you wanted to hear. The key to success is to be able to listen to fair criticism and ACT ON IT without taking things too personally. Listen with an open mind to your ideal client, and be prepared to flex your initial ideas until what you're offering becomes EXACTLY what they need!

> **MINDSHIFT - BE THE DECISION MAKER,
> BE TRANSPARENT AND BE LEVEL WITH REALITY**

One of the great parts of building your own legacy business is that awesome feeling that finally, you are the boss. There is no-one else calling the shots.

What this also means, is that there is no-one telling you what to do. Now for most people, this is great news, especially when things are all going well. The flipside is that there is also no-one telling you what to do when you have difficult decisions to make!

So take the lead, and don't be afraid to make decisions. It is almost always better to take control and take action, rather than sitting back and letting things happen TO you.

The buck DOES stop with you, so you'll also need to be able to be responsible for the choices you make. If things don't go right, don't fall into the trap of looking for people to blame. Look at your own actions, look at what is, or was, under your control, and figure out a plan for what to do differently next time. Every perceived 'failure' is an opportunity to be better next time after all.

MINDSHIFT - PAY THE PRICE!

Being realistic about what your budgets are at the start is a really important part of communicating well with your creatives. It's all very well having amazing mood boards, fantastic creative ideas, a huge vision for your shoot and a brief for hundreds of images for a new campaign every week, you want, but if your budget is in reality only going to cover half a day of your creative's time, it's likely that EVERYONE is going to end up disappointed in some way or other!

It's ok to aim high, but you need to be realistic about your expectations, and how much they will cost to achieve.

MINDSHIFT - AGREE ON OUTCOMES

A good creative partner should be able to guide your clearly through what they are able to deliver for your timescale and your budget. Think about what deliverables you actually want to achieve, and set these out clearly at the start. Are your images print, or digital? How many images do you need? When do you need the final images by, and is that achievable with your schedule?

MINDSHIFT - AGREE ON REVISIONS AND THE PROCESS AROUND THIS

Now it's fair to say that not everyone gets everything they ever do right first time. Because of the nature of creative work, and what we've already seen about how open things can be to interpretation, there ARE likely to be times when you need to work with your creative on revisions, or amends.

The key to this not causing problems is to make sure you discuss the process around this at the start, BEFORE the work takes place. You can ask your creative what their policy is on allowing client revisions. How many rounds of amends, if any, do they include as standard? If revisions or amends are chargeable, what rates normally apply? Are there any small types of amends which they would NOT normally charge for e.g. correcting a tiny typo perhaps, or switching out one image for another.

Staying open in communications like this really does pay off, and will make any issues a lot smoother to manager further down the line.

MINDSHIFT - BE AWARE OF TIME ZONES

We've mentioned being clear in the brief about when you expect the deliverables you agree on with your creative. For example, if you need something done 'by Tuesday', do you mean you want to be using it in a mailout at 9am on Tuesday morning? Or is it fine to have it land, completed, in your inbox by the end of the day, ready for you to use on Wednesday? The more specific you can be when you discuss your expectations the better!

Another thing which you might not have considered before is working with creative or others in different time zones to you. The internet, skype and video calling, instant messaging and project sharing apps mean that you don't always need to physically be face to face with someone to be present with them. I've worked with clients across multiple countries and time zones in the past, and considering creative people from all over the world will really widen the net, and also possibly influence a wider understanding of all the great things you could achieve when you start to think more globally.

If you do work with people overseas, keep in mind that your early morning may be their late night. Be sensitive to this - not many people want to be woken up at 3am to discuss work because the client hasn't realised the time zone difference when they called! Be realistic about response times too with this in mind.

Trans-time zone relationships can really work in your favour if you're smart about how you work. Have an assistant who is just waking up as you clock off for the day? Make sure you've fully briefed them with all the relevant info they will need, and you can wake up the next day to find everything is already taken care of!

SUMMARY

So we've covered a lot here on how to get the best out of your relationship with your lovely creative. Finding the right person to work with to bring your dreams to life is an exciting process.

As long as your creative is FULLY ALIGNED to your brand vision, your dreamy client and YOU, then you'll have all the right ingredients to create stunning visuals for your STAND OUT BRAND!

PART 7

MEET THE WOMEN WHO MADE SIX FIGURES FROM THEIR SHOOTS

Creating a solid, legacy business that is going to stand the test of time, ride the waves of economic change and hold strong during the ups and downs of life is not easy. Crafting a STAND OUT brand that resonates so deeply with your ideal client is the key to having a legacy business, and as we have spent the last few chapters looking at in detail, your images, graphics and photos play a HUGE role in communicating with your target market.

I'd like to introduce you to three fabulous women. These women have not only built multiple six figure businesses, but have also fallen in love with being in front of the camera. They now harness the power of "incredible" photography to strengthen their brand and cement themselves a legacy.

Linda

I'm Linda Morrison, a fitness and life coach, and I've been a coach all my working life.

I got my business online about four or five years ago with no computer knowledge whatsoever - I did not even know how to open my MacBook Pro when I started out! I realized that coaching was going to be the best way to help more people without me working like crazy killing myself as a physical trainer.

I'd also gone through a divorce, we'd separated. The money was cut. I had to learn to be a bread winner overnight and I didn't want to leave my children for hours and hours every day.

They had always had me.

I'd always worked, but I had never been away from the children for whole days before, so it just didn't compute with me that I would do that. So that's why I developed an online presence and a bigger, better brand. I needed the ability to own my intellectual property more so.

I knew that my brand only had moments to impress people online. In the physical world, I had no problem with my teaching skills, communication, my warmth, getting to know people, meeting people, all of those sorts of things. However, I knew as soon as it went online that you actually had to do all of that in just moments.

I very quickly learnt that you cannot, without good branding and good photographs, communicate to your audience. The photographs and everything else which comes with that branding is paramount. You will not stand out unless it's good. It doesn't matter how good you are at your craft if you do not stand out amongst the masses. They won't see you anyway.

So, the photographs have to be the right photographs.

The messaging around it, around you has to be just right.

It has to express a mood that you would normally be able to express when you present yourself in person. Looking the part is very important of course in the fitness and wellness industry I was in. Health attracts, so you have to look healthy in order to attract people who want to invest in health.

The most important thing is that I knew my target market. My target market is women over 40 who want to lose weight and get more energy. Which is just about 70% or more of women here in Australia and then of course the wider western world, which is where my business has grown to.

In the last five years I've written five books for my target market, which I'm very proud of, and again the books have evolved as I've evolved. They are for busy women over 40, but it doesn't mean that any of these concepts are irrelevant if you're under 40 - if you're busy and a woman, they're relevant! I knew that I wanted to keep refining who I was talking to, and it was the same with my pictures and photography as well. The pictures have evolved over time.

What I found was my initial photographs were very fitness-y.

They were probably appealing to a younger market because I looked younger. As I have evolved over the time I've been growing my business, the shots I use have become much subtler, but still show that you're fit and healthy.

They're not shots just with abdominals out, or pictures in very tight clothing. It's all much more tasteful, much more beautiful. It's how women tell me they'd like to look at the end after working with me.

And that's how I wanted to photograph myself, casually in jeans, in a nice dress, all those sorts of things.

I definitely underestimated the quality of photographs that I needed at first. They have got better and better as I've developed. I make a commitment to get more images every year; better images, to allow me to keep conveying, keep communicating.

Here are the top tips I have learnt:

Trust your photographer to lead you.

Definitely, definitely, definitely have an idea of what you want the mode or the feel to be like.

Work with your photographer to tell them, and get them to help you with working out how to convey that.

I think connection through images is very, very, very important in this online world. Because that moment of looking at a picture does convey a million things, and it is that video and that photography that says so much more than just words alone. I don't know that people read all that much online, but I think when you connect to them in pictures, and in some video, if you're there with them that goes a lot further than spending time in scribing. It's not that your IP and writing down your stuff isn't important, but these images are just so, so important.

As my experience with using photographs in my business is evolving I am getting more comfortable with the idea that you need regular shoots, like the way you see editorials in magazines. Your clients and your customers want to see you! They want constant flow, be it clients you are working with already, or new clients who are finding you online. I think that we don't always realize the responsibility of this - people want your photos!

They literally say to me 'When are you getting new photos?!' or, 'I love this photo of you, you should do *this*!". They offer me advice, which I think is gorgeous and beautiful, because they see different things in me. It's what attracts them to my business. It's connecting with them on a very personable level.

So, for me, as a very practical coach (and hopefully a good one!) I have a creative freedom about me in my business. I can actually go on the journey of creating this next branding experience, this next photographic journey, from the ideas and the suggestions of the people I am working with - from the clients I am attracting to my business - so that the images resonate, and speak directly to them. Every new set of photographs that comes through my brand is more and more led by what the clients see in me.

I knew I wouldn't stand out unless I had a great brand. I've researched other people in the wellness industry, the health industry, the fitness industry and beyond. Some of them are doctors and things like that, and people will say to me, 'Oh did you read other professionals / chiropractors / my mate's / physiotherapists' / so and so's article on this?' I'll say I didn't, because I find them boring.

I have a wellness transformation brand. I haven't been sticking to the photos that everybody else in that brand area has actually done with a great big bag of vegetables. It absolutely has not been the way I've decided to go. Finding your own way that conveys your particular brand and IP plus a good branding photographer will help you with this. It's very, very important.

Bunmi

My name is Bunmi and I'm a recovery coach. I help professionals and addicts, professionals who are addicts, or struggling with addiction, to become sober.

I built my business from the ground up, and it's now online. What I found though was as soon as I'd built the website, everybody just says how beautiful it is, because the photography and the branding really make it stand out.

When I started out, I was thinking, "Oh, I don't know what to do with the branding." So, getting some help and taking time to look at the colours, look at who your target market is, and everything else, was absolutely the most valuable use of my time especially now seeing what has been created from doing that.

I've had the exact response I was hoping for to the site. I knew the stigma for recovery coaching would be a very clinical looking, NHS-type appearance, so I wanted to really go away from this. The response I get is "It's warm, private, professional, high end, trustworthy." Which is exactly what I was looking for.

As my services aren't just about allocating you a counsellor and then talking at each scheduled appointment for exactly 60 minutes, I wanted my branding to evoke exactly what I provide - which is a *partnership* with the client, helping them move forward. Helping people find their own pathways forward, proactively in a committed professional, private and warm way.

My branding journey has been a complete learning curve. I sort of had to work out our brand advantage, and it quickly became apparent the industry is not very personable, so I thought, "Well, that's the standard." Looking at my target market, they are professional people. They work very busy hours, things are very hectic. And they probably want somebody that they can turn to and who can help in the most difficult times, which might mean me having to go to them at six o'clock in the morning because they've got a big business meeting that day, and they're flying out of the country. So I started looking at it and thinking, "My target market is this." Really visualizing who and what it was. That's when I started to be able to create what I created.

One of the biggest tips I have learnt is that it's really important to communicate with creatives who are helping you in your business. Pick your website, pick your web designers. They're *you*! Really make sure you gel, and that they understand completely what you are looking for and who you are looking to work with.

My relationship with my designer is at the point where we just reach out, and we resonate, and they can see my bigger picture. It's really important for someone to be able to see what is possible. They need to understand your vision, so that they can feel that and interpret it.

The first experience of a photo shoot I had was in Santorini! I was just thrilled, I looked at little bits of it, like traveling to Santorini, and choosing the clothes that I was going to wear, I was choosing carefully what suited me. What jewellery I was gonna wear, I was really excited. I knew that for these images I wanted a very professional look. I wanted the world to see that woman, who looks professional, warm, and think "she looks friendly and great." So, I was really excited, and it was really good. I loved it.

I quickly learnt I needed to have pictures of me taken regularly, for example at events, and do photo shoots in different outfits. I realised it spoke directly to my clients, as if saying that 'This person has a life as well. I'm ten years in recovery, and this is what I've achieved, this is what you can achieve'. You have to show up and BE the ambassador for the services you are providing and the transformation you are offering.

I have found that my branding has made me feel organised. I know I have everything I need to take this business to wherever I want it to go. I know what we're going to put out for the year in terms of campaigns, who we're going to target with our PR, so the branding helps clarify all those areas as well.

Having a strong brand identity really helps me to see the bigger picture of my business. It helps me to almost put things into, 'that'll work, that won't work' categories. I've got this portfolio of fonts and colours and photographs together and now it makes me feel it is mine, it feels valued. I cherish it more. Building your brand is like having babies - you want to make sure your baby's got the right clothes on at the right time. You feel proud of it!

Vanessa

I'm Vanessa Moss. I help coaches, consultants, and entrepreneurs to write and publish their books and become best-selling authors so that they are positioned as experts in their industry.

I started out in the health and fitness industry. I transitioned from health and fitness into helping coaches in the health and fitness industry to grow their businesses. Then I naturally progressed into books because I just saw that all of my clients wanted to write books.

With my health and fitness business, it was targeted at mums whose children were five and above; the kids have gone back to school and they are looking to get themselves back to health.

When I started to brand the business, I really understood what that market was. It was called Yummy Mummy. I didn't want something too pretty, or girly, but I wanted something that still spoke to that female audience.

From there my businesses transitioned into higher paying clients and into books and it became more about positioning it to people.

I understood that within my branding, it was almost like I had to become the person that my clients wanted to be. So my branding became more about a successful female entrepreneur that was positioned in herself, and in her industry.

I quickly realised I was going to need to have branding photographs taken. I hadn't had photographs for years, never had a professional shoot. I hadn't got any images, apart from perhaps something that I'd taken on my phone. I was seeing more and more of the people in my industry having the same kind of stuff all the time. Someone skipping down the street, or the Eiffel Tower, for example. I knew I wanted my shoot to say 'success', 'wealth', but also 'lifestyle' as well, because I understood that my people wanted to be seen as experts in their industry, but I didn't want to rock on up in a suit and make it look really, really corporate.

I'd really niched down on my clients in my books. Before, it was men and women, but I was just getting about 90% women now coming through wanting their books. So I decided to really make my branding and those shoots really feminine, and speak directly to those women. That's when I started to realize that I needed to step up and get these different types of images, to stand out from everyone else who was trying to position themselves at the same time.

My first shoot experience was horrible. The person that I booked with didn't go through anything with me. They never went through anything for prep or clothes or anything like that. I just rocked on up with the outfits I thought would work, and it was all a bit off. I must say when I got all the photos back I was only happy with one of them. I think that's because there was no preparation and I didn't feel comfortable.

It made me want to do another shoot, but to get booked to work with the right person and then get that help from that person. I knew next time I would really go to work on what I was going to wear, and get Pinterest boards together of what poses I was going to do.

I believe that you've got to keep having a turnover of images. I see people using the same images. They'll have this shoot and then you'll see their images for four, six, eight weeks but then they keep using them and using them and using them and you get bored. You're bored of seeing that picture and so is your client!

My biggest tip for anyone planning to use photography in their business is to keep on top of the imagery. You need amazing quality pictures, but you need that good turnover of pictures as well, because your client's mind just gets bored if they're not seeing that new, updated stuff all the time.

STAND OUT BRANDS - OVER TO YOU!!

Whether you're launching in a new direction, finally stepping up to own your genius or simply taking your business to the stars; utilising photography in your business will achieve you your dreams so much more quickly.

Connecting your target audience emotionally and fanatically, to create a celebrity must-have brand is the ultimate goal.

More recognition equals...

        more impact, equals...

                more people helped.

Don't sit in the fear of standing tall. Be BOLD, speaking your truth and creating emotional bonds with your tribe.

Don't make the mistake of thinking one image of you is all they need.

They crave you. They crave knowing you, seeing you, feeling you, so that they can feel safe and comfortable knowing you are the solution to their most pressing problem.

Use images to your advantage, think outside of the box and get creative with positioning your expertise.

Darling, don't follow the crowd.

Put on your crown.

Show up.

Shine bright...

STAND OUT!!!

www.ingramcontent.com/pod-product-compliance
Lightning Source LLC
Chambersburg PA
CBHW032211220526
45472CB00018B/856